Creative Comfort

Creative Comfort

Where Grief Meets God

NATALIE WEEDMAN

CREATIVE ENTERPRISES STUDIO

BEDFORD, TEXAS

Published in association with Books, Bach & Beyond, Inc. d/b/a Creative Enterprises Studio, 1507 Shirley Way, Suite A, Bedford, TX 76022. CreativeEnterprisesStudio.com.

Library of Congress Control Number 2023919080
ISBN: 97989876583-7-6
Cover Design: StudioAnneli.com
Printed in the United States of America
23 24 25 26 27 28   KDP   6 5 4 3 2 1

Dedication

DEDICATION

Graham Wesley

The apple of our eye, our little man, our Bubba. To the one who made us parents and taught us depths of love that we couldn't imagine without you. In life you brought us so much joy; in passing you have connected others to our hope in Jesus. We can't wait to see you again and smother you with all the hugs and kisses you missed out on earth-side (and would have tried to squirm out of). We love you always, buddy. Thank you for changing our lives forever.

Jesse

A few weeks after Graham passed, I remember we found one of his tiny socks stuffed in some cranny in the backseat of our car. First we chuckled. Graham was always taking off his socks in the car when we weren't looking. Then we teared up. You kissed that sock and stuck it in your pocket that day. To the man who still carries that sock in his pocket: I love you. Thanks for being the best dad to Graham. On a funnier note, I never knew that someone could stuff so many things in a diaper bag "just in case." Thanks for being the extra-prepared one of us. More than once, you saved the day.

Our Tribe

I wish I could even attempt to write all the names of the people who spoke a word at the right time, who prayed for us, who stood with us, who cried with us. It has impacted us, it has changed us, it has encouraged and strengthened us. How can we ever repay the Lord and others for this precious work? May we be those who build the Body of Christ in turn.

Our Favorite Photos

Contents

Prologue

About a year after Graham passed away, I was in my living room early one morning. I had just finished up my devotional time and was about to head upstairs and get ready for the day. As I was moving toward the lamp to switch it off, I heard a clear, firm voice speak to my heart: "You are going to write a book." It stopped me in my tracks. *A book?* I thought. I could have laughed. *What could I possibly have to write about, Lord?* I didn't have answers for anyone. I didn't even have answers for myself. Like Jacob in Genesis, I felt as if I had been thrown into a wrestle of a lifetime with no idea how I got there. My son was gone. My world was upside down. The only thing I knew to do was to latch onto the Lord with all my might. "You're going to write about how you walked through grief with me," was the answer. *Okay, Lord.* That felt hopeful. It spoke of work the Lord had yet to do in my heart. *Please just help me know when the time is right.*

A few years later I was again in my living room when the Lord spoke to me a second time, this time in a more surprising way. I was scrolling through social media and interacting with a few accounts I followed. One such account was of a Christian influencer who I knew to be a woman of faith and a powerful prayer warrior. One of her posts about prayer really impacted me, and I made a comment about how much I loved it. To my surprise, she responded a few minutes later, completely off topic: "The Lord said you are supposed to start writing a book this year."

What? I did not know this woman personally, nor had I told anyone about what God had spoken to me years before. Hello confirmation! *All right Lord,* here we go. That week I opened a blank note in my iPhone and began writing.

As this book began to take shape, the theme of creative comfort began to emerge. I found God focusing me, not only on the grief processing, but also how he ministered to me in creative and personal ways as I included him in it. I would venture to say that most Christians can recite by heart many of the comfort Scriptures. However, I am not so sure we access the full spectrum of God's very real and tangible comfort that is available to us. Maybe it's because there are few times in our lives when we need it so pointedly as when we are walking through grief. Or maybe it's because we are used to hearing about creativity in other realms but not so much in grief. Isn't grief just something we endure? Of course, we know God cares, but do we actually let him in as close as he wants to be? Do we let him go to those deep places of hurt and turmoil with us in ways that allow us to grieve with complete freedom? Do we see how he is reaching out to us in unique and personal ways? Are we leaning into him and placing a demand on him to be everything the Bible tells us he is? Do we really, actually know him as a creative Comforter?

I think some of our practical hang-ups in grief are more easily seen when compared with how different cultures grieve. In some Eastern cultures and Judaism specifically, grieving is something physical and active. Even in Jesus's day, people actually paid others in their community to grieve with them. They would put on quite a spectacle in an outward display of grief, weeping and wailing along with the family. Even today practicing Jews spend months and years completing certain types of grief activities, including dressing in certain ways. Physical outlets and outward signs of grief are expected. There is something to do.

Now compare that to Western culture. Beyond the visitation, wake, or funeral, there is really no structure, no idea of "so what now?" I probably don't have to tell you that processing grief is not as intuitive as you might think. That is why so many feel that coping or numbing their pain is their only option. Did God give us great tools like wise counselors, therapists, and prescription medication? Yes. Were those things meant to replace the presence of God in your grief journey? Absolutely not. I would venture to say that not tapping into that in our grief journey only adds to our grief. Injury is the loss of a loved one. Insult to injury is quiet desperation without access to true, meaningful comfort.

In my own grief journey, I have felt the deepest depths of gut-wrenching anguish and pain. I have known what it is like to cry out to God and scream into pillows. To have nothing left of myself. Grief is not something you even begin to comprehend until you're in it. It's like getting married or becoming a parent. People can tell you about it, you can read about it, but until you experience it, someone else's commentary on what it's like is such a 2D version of a 4D immersive reality.

On the other hand, I have also experienced the deep comfort and presence of God that has absolutely changed my life. I have walked into moments with the Lord one way and walked out completely different. I have had dreams, seen visions, and received revelatory words from others that have made me feel seen by God and changed my perspective. It's not about making grief go away, as if that were possible. It is about expecting and receiving something from God that is weightier and deeper than grief, without dictating to him how he needs to do it. It's about allowing your spiritual imagination to be turned on and realize that God is not limited by our grief. This is when I began to know God as a creative Comforter, and I was left to marvel at all the ways he displayed his nature in my grief journey.

Chances are you have picked up this book because you or someone you love is walking the grief journey right now. I truly believe you are reading this book on purpose. I have prayed for you! And to you I say what someone else said to me in the beginning: welcome to the club that no one wants to be in.

Maybe, like me, you know there is something more for you than just reminding yourself that your loved one is "in a better place" or trying to pacify your inner turmoil with comforting Scripture. Don't get me wrong, I absolutely believe in heaven and the Bible as the ultimate source of truth. How we need it as our foundation! But unless our knowledge of Scripture translates into revelation in our hearts and minds through the Holy Spirit, knowing it in theory won't help us. Pretending that it does is like putting a Band-Aid on a gaping wound. It doesn't work in the natural, and it doesn't work in the spiritual either.

I feel like it is really important to mention that grief is not limited to loss of a loved one. There are many people who have experienced grief, trauma, distress, and turmoil in other ways. Maybe it's known to those around you, or maybe it's not. Maybe you fully understand why you feel the way you do, or maybe you don't. If that's you, know that God wanted me to mention it specifically for a reason. You are not left out of creative comfort! The circumstances may be different but our need for real help from our Heavenly Father is the same. I pray that this helps you and encourages you as you are walking out your own healing journey.

Although I was not always the best reader, there were two books that really encouraged me in my own grief journey. The first was written by a mother who had lost her teen daughter Ashley when she was struck and killed by a car. Although I can't remember the title of the book (despite much online searching), what stood out to me is how this mother took her questions to the Lord as she processed her grief. As she did God began to answer her through Scripture, through unique dreams and visions, and through encouraging—even prophetic—words from believers around her. Not only did it open my eyes to some of the ways God was creatively reaching out to me with his comfort, it encouraged me to open up my heart even more to any way he may want to express it.

The second book that was incredibly encouraging to me in my grief journey is *Imagine Heaven* by John Burke. This was given to me by a friend not long after Graham passed. The book itself is full of stories about people who have near-death experiences and see heaven. Many of them meet Jesus and talk about how it felt to be near him. I did not use the book as a basis of theology, but rather as a tool to expand my God imagination. One of the passages that really struck my heart was the account of a woman named Hazeliene from Singapore who went to heaven after she "blacked out, hit her head," and apparently "died." She tells her story in English, which is not her native language:

I suddenly was in the very dark tunnel going up, up, up . . . After passing through from that very dark tunnel, it has changed to very bright light. I had seen a very bright light, I thought it was sun, but it was not. I don't have an idea where that light came from. Someone spoke to me for a while, I heard, and that voice came from that light. You know what I felt when I saw that light?

When I saw that bright light, I felt that someone loves me very much (but no idea who it was). I was very overwhelmed with that bright light. And while I was there, I felt the love, and that love I never felt before. That light welcoming me very warmly and loves me very much. My word to the light before I [revived] was this: *I wanted to stay here, but I love my two kids.* When I said this, I suddenly woke up ... Was it true that the light was GOD? Reason why I felt very overwhelmed? I felt that only that light ever love me and no one does. All people know only to beat me, hurt me, criticized me, offended me and many more. Nobody love me like that kind of love before. How I wish my two kids and me could go there and feel that love forever.[1]

Even though it did not specifically talk about grief, it gave a lot of color around what I imagined Graham to be experiencing in heaven. As a parent, your biggest concern on earth is that your child is safe and loved. Although I knew Graham was now in the safest place possible, when I read other people's accounts of their experiences—what they saw, felt and experienced—it opened up an avenue of comfort in my grief journey. Graham was getting to experience an overwhelming love that mere human (even parental) emotion could not even begin to touch. He knew the love of God in its overwhelming fullness. What I always knew to be true from the word of God dropped into my heart with greater revelation.

Ultimately what impacted me most about these books were the stories. A dear friend and pastor often says, "Your testimony [story] is someone else's prophecy." In other words, hearing what God did for someone else increases my faith to believe he can do it for me too! Stories are what change our lives. Stories are what give us hope. I don't think it co-incidence that the Bible is full of stories, out of which we draw useful lessons and application for our lives. Some have the application spelled out, some you have to seek out like a treasure. It's possible that some of the things I talk about in this book may be new ideas for you. I encourage you to prayerfully seek out the kernel of truth that God is trying to show you. Chances are that it may just confirm something you have been sensing in your heart already.

More than anything, I pray that as you read the story of my own journey of walking through grief with God that you begin to see God's hand at work in your own life. He wants to reveal his character and his nature to you. He wants to walk with you. He wants to bring comfort to you in unique, creative, and meaningful ways. He wants to help you. He wants to fill you. He wants you to see that even though the hurt goes deep, the depth of his comfort and love goes deeper still.

Chapter 1

The Beginning

—◯

As I started to write, the question of how to begin the story of Graham was one of the hardest for me to think about. Should I start at his birth? Should I just give a little history and then tell the story of the last few days leading up to his life? Graham was only with us for a little over fourteen months, but the moments and memories feel endless. The more I thought and prayed about it, the more I felt that knowing the context of my life is important as well. So I'll step back a little further in time and start there.

Growing up, I had a pretty normal Christian life. I was the oldest of four girls. My parents were pastors in the small rural Midwest town we lived in. I had average grades, slightly below average sporting abilities, and a real desire to serve the Lord and do something with my life.

Although I didn't personally feel called to the ministry like my parents, I was sure that putting God first was the right thing to do and ultimately the way I wanted to live my life. The only problem was I had a lot of head knowledge about God but I didn't actually know him that well. Because of that, what should have been a great childhood on paper was addled by a lot of anger, depression, anxiety, and many years of battling with eating disorders.

One of the wonderful things about being a pastor's kid was that all of my sisters and I would usually go to out-of-town church conferences with my parents. I remember being in eighth grade or so when we went to a conference in a very small town in the middle of Missouri, called Smithton. My parents had heard from a pastor friend of theirs that this church was experiencing an outpouring of the Holy Spirit, or a revival.

"Revival services" are a weekend of intensive church services with a special speaker that are usually marked by many salvations. However, in this context, "revival" meant that people who had been serving the Lord for a long time were receiving something fresh from the Holy Spirit, which was characterized by exuberant praise and worship, convicting messages, and testimonies of people's lives being changed, including healings and addictions being broken.

I will never forget stepping foot into that service during the worship time, all at once feeling overwhelmed, awed, and a little afraid. It was the first time I had felt the presence of God with such intensity. The music was loud, yes, but something happened in my spirit. Rationally I had always known that God was bigger than my problems and personal hang-ups, but for the first time I actually *felt* it. Something in my heart said, *This is what you have been looking for!* Fast forward through the next few years, and my parents continued to periodically visit this revival and bring us girls along. Every time we did, it reconfirmed what my heart told me in that first service. By the time I graduated from high school, I had made a decision to attend their school of ministry, which by that time was located in Kansas City. It wasn't the most comfortable decision to leave my whole life behind, but I wanted my life to change and I wanted to put myself in an environment where that could happen.

The two years in the school of ministry were intense and amazing. In addition to school all week, I was also attending church services four days per week. Life was busy and full, but I wouldn't have it any other way. I was being immersed in the things of God, and for the first time I really felt like my spirit was really coming alive! My life was far from perfect, but I was beginning to see the good fruit of investing my life into the things of God. I was being changed from the inside out! Initially I had thought that I would move on to another city after my time in the school of ministry, but I decided to stay in Kansas City. I liked where my life was heading in God, and I really felt like I had found my tribe.

As time went on I became more settled as a young adult but was still very active in my church community. It was where I ended up meeting my future husband, Jesse. I will never forget talking to him for the first time. I actually felt the Lord actually say in my spirit, "Are you ready to start this?" The rest, you could say, is history. Not only was Jesse a man who loved the Lord with all his heart, he had an amazing and large family whom I loved.

Jesse and I were married in May 2010 and started a new life together. Over the next few years we talked on and off about having kids but had never really made the decision to go for it until 2014. Growing up, I didn't think I wanted kids, but over the years something in my heart had changed. Now I was about to embark on a journey I never thought I would be on. I like to think that I was prepared for it, but out of the two of us, I think Jesse had read more parenting books!

One of the books we read together was *The Power of Blessing Your Children* by Mary Ruth Swope. It was a book my mom had given us, written by a grandmother who modeled prayers for her grandchildren after the blessings the patriarchs declared over their offspring in the Bible. The idea is that by speaking blessings over their children, parents bestow godly identity and shape their future. This is a common theme in Jewish texts, and even Jesus received audible blessings from his Father at different points in his ministry. "This is my Son, whom I love; with him I am well pleased." (Matt. 3:17). A blessing! We were determined that we would be parents who not only raised their kids but blessed their kids with godly identity. The months leading up to Graham's birth were full of prayer and declarations. Even in the womb, we started blessing that kid!

On a personal level I had a lot of nervous excitement. I will never forget how, one day, I was praying while getting ready for the day and thinking about our son. *What would he be like? Who was he going to be in God? Were we going to be good parents? I don't want to mess this kid up! Lord, help us to raise him right!* This was not an uncommon track of thought in those early days of pregnancy.

I will never forget that, as I was pondering these things, the Lord interrupted my thoughts: "This will be the child of promise that you are looking for." It stopped me in my tracks. To this day I still remember exactly where I was when he spoke that word to me. Something in my heart and expectations changed that day. I took that word to heart: Graham was going to be a child of promise to us, just as Isaac was to Abraham.

When Graham was born, the first thing we noticed was how alert he was. That kid kept his eyes open for almost every single visitor who came to see him that night! We chuckle about it to this day. He just didn't want to miss anything! He was so calm and content, too, something we had prayed about before he was born. As we settled into a new life as a family of three, we went through the same growing pains that everyone does. Sleep deprivation, life revolving around nap and eating schedules. But no matter how hectic life felt, we felt so blessed by this gift from God.

Since Jesse and I worked for the same company, we were able to coordinate our parental leave in such a way that we were able to keep Graham at home for about three months. It was one of the greatest gifts, and it was so fun to see Jesse experience some of the same bonding time as I did. Going back to work was difficult for both of us (although I really missed adult company!) but one of the things I loved to witness was Jesse bless Graham every time we dropped him off at his babysitter's. We would walk in with Graham in the car seat. Jesse would set him down on the floor and then get down on his level. He would look at him and pray and declare what a good day he was going to have, that it was going to be peaceful and safe. That he was going to eat and sleep well. We had several babysitters in the time that Graham was with us, and all of them told us how much they loved watching Graham being blessed. This was our custom every day and at night when Graham went to bed.

Watching Graham's personality develop was fascinating. Before he was born, Jesse and I would joke that we had no idea what kind of personality he was going to have because I come from a family of introverts and Jesse came from a family of extroverts. Honestly though, I think Graham got the best of both sides. That kid could express himself with the best of them but when he was interested in a certain toy, he would sit in concentration for many minutes, looking at the details, and pushing any moving parts that he could to see what happened.

As Graham grew we noticed how much he liked to jabber and talk. When he was four months old, we witnessed his first "baby rant." Jesse had just finished changing his diaper and was holding him when Graham looked at both of us and began to jabber in such a way that sounded like a lecture. We even heard an "I love you" in there too! This probably went on for almost a minute and we laughed and laughed. We weren't sure what this kid was going to be when he grew up, but we definitely knew he would not lack any words!

Later, just four days before he passed away, he had woken up especially early one Sunday morning. I'll never forget waking up to that sunshine; it was the end of May and the mornings were bright and beautiful. Most times I would have wished for Graham to sleep in, but that morning was different. I was going to leave later that morning to go on a work trip to Zurich, Switzerland; this would be the first time I would be away from Graham for this long. I remember feeling excited that we got some extra time together, and I went to get him out of his crib. We came downstairs and into our kitchen and I fixed him some breakfast. Oatmeal was the choice of the day. He was in such a talkative mood. At almost fifteen months old, he was, of course, saying *mama* and *dada*, but that morning he was practicing his intonation and inflection with several minutes of confident gibberish. I couldn't turn on my phone to record it fast enough, I had learned as a mom to keep my phone handy in case my kid did something adorable, which in my opinion was quite often. But this moment felt extra special. He was truly "telling me all about it" and going on and on. We finished breakfast, at which point "dada" woke up and took over so I could finish my packing and they could get ready for church.

When it was time for them to leave for church, I hugged and kissed them both, told Graham I loved him and then went upstairs to continue packing while Jesse got him buckled into the car seat outside. It felt so strange to be saying goodbye to my son for almost a full week.

With that thought, I went back downstairs and out the door to give Graham and Jesse one last hug and kiss before they left the driveway. In hindsight, I am thankful that I had the chance to squeeze the last drop out of what I didn't know would be the last time I saw Graham face to face.

The next few days of travel and meetings went well, and I checked in with Jesse as time and the time difference would allow. Both he and the babysitter would send me pictures throughout the day. I remember specifically coming back to the hotel after dinner on May 24, really missing them both but knowing Jesse was at work and Graham was at the sitter's.

Completely uncharacteristic of me, I thought "I should record a video of myself to tell them how much I miss them!" I recorded it sitting on my bed in my hotel room. I told Graham that I missed him so much and that I loved him and that I couldn't wait to see him. What is oh so precious to me is that, when Jesse played it for Graham the next day, he recorded Graham's reaction watching it. It was the sweetest thing. I will never forget the expressions on his face as he looked at the screen with a shy and beaming smile, then looked at daddy, then back at the screen again. In hindsight I know that the Holy Spirit prompted me to do that and prompted Jesse to capture his response on video.

Back in the conference room in Zurich, we had a short break, and I got online to check Facebook and see what was going on in the States. Immediately my eyes landed on a post from my brother-in-law that said something to the effect of, "Please pray, Graham is having trouble with his breathing."

Immediately I felt my stomach drop to my shoes and my heart began to race. What is going on? I thought as I simultaneously grabbed my phone and got up to walk out of the room. I called Jesse twice from the hall outside the room. People were passing by, speaking pleasantly with their colleagues as I waited for him to pick up. No answer.

I then called my mother-in-law, Sherry, to see if she knew what was going on. Despite being in a different state, she had likely seen the post, too, and I figured she was involved in some way. I called her once. No answer. On the second try, she picked up the phone and I could tell in her voice she had been crying. I told her I had seen the post, asked her what was going on, was Graham okay, and so on. She said, "I am going to pass the phone to Jesse, okay?"

In that moment my mind began to race. Was Graham in the hospital? Was there something seriously wrong? Then Jesse spoke, his voice also betraying the fact he had been crying. That is when I knew.

"Natalie, I am so sorry but Graham passed away. We don't know what happened, but he passed away last night." His voice cracked and he broke down. "I'm so sorry. I'm so sorry." I could feel a wave of shock sweep over my body. My heart was beating loud and my mouth dried up. *What? Passed away?? How? What had happened?* Almost not comprehending what I had just been told, I started asking questions. When did Jesse find him? Was he responsive?

First, I found out why Jesse had not initially answered my call: he was unaware of my brother-in-law's post and he had not wanted to break the news to me while I was overseas. However when I kept calling, he realized that was not an option. Jesse went on to tell me everything had gone as normal when he had put Graham to bed the night before. Jesse woke up the next morning and checked the monitor to see that Graham was still asleep, so he had gone down to prepare his breakfast. When he walked into the room to get Graham, he knew something was wrong. Graham didn't stand up in his crib like he normally did in the morning. When Jesse called his name and touched him, he did not respond. Jesse scooped him up and raced to the hospital, holding Graham to his chest the entire way. Jesse drove up to the hospital door, rushed out of his car with Graham and ran inside.

"My son isn't breathing!" he told them. The doctors took Graham immediately and tried to resuscitate him but could not bring him back.

At that point I couldn't speak, I just cried, hot tears running down my cheeks. However even in that moment I felt the Holy Spirit take over my thoughts and turn them back to Jesse. How must he feel? He was all alone when that happened, and I could only imagine the voices of guilt he was dealing with. Immediately I said, "Jesse, this is not your fault, okay? I am going to come home, and we are going to figure this out, okay? I love you. I don't know what to say except, "Lord, help us. We don't know what to do, but our eyes are on you."

I hung up the phone in a daze. My eyes darted around the hallways and adjoining conference rooms. I felt like I wanted to run, to throw up, and to scream all at once. What was happening, what was I supposed to do? I couldn't even tell my body to move. At that moment, two colleagues who were in the workshop with me walked up to me and smiled, "How's it going?" I was at a loss. My voice cracked and trembled "I just found out my son passed away."

Immediately I saw his countenance change with shock as his eyes widened. "Oh, my God. I am so sorry," he said hurriedly, motioning for me to stay there while he grabbed the workshop leader. The workshop leader quickly came out along with my colleague. They ushered me over to the break room while my things were gathered from the conference room, and I sat down in shock. This couldn't be real. This wasn't real.

Bringing me back to the present, my colleague gave me a giant hug and began to pray for me. There are nice prayers and there are powerful prayers, and this was the latter. Tears began to stream even more. Even in my shock and grief I knew that God himself was ministering to me in that moment through my colleague. He prayed until my things were retrieved from the conference room and we were rushed out the door. Outside a driver was waiting to take us to the hotel to pick up my things and put me on a plane back home. He assured me they were rearranging flights for me, so all I needed to do was walk in and get on the plane.

I got to the hotel, quickly packed my things, and stepped into the car. Unfortunately, it took about forty-five minutes to get to the airport, and it was rush hour. The driver seemed uneasy about my arriving on time. When I arrived at the airport, we found out that his uneasiness was justified. I had missed my flight, and the next flight was not available for twenty-four hours. I cried again. All I wanted to do was be home.

Thankfully there was a hotel attached to the airport, so I decided to book a room there that night. However, before I did so I knew I needed to call my parents to let them know what had happened. I was full of dread. How do you even break news like this? Lord, help me. They knew I was in Zurich, so any request to talk now was probably to sound strange. I sat down in a quiet nook in the airport and texted my parents: "Do you both have time to chat together?" It was about 4:00 p.m. Zurich time, which meant it was 10:00 a.m. in the Midwest. They said they had time, so I called.

I think I started off the call with "How are you?" and they asked me the same. I can't remember what I said in the first few seconds, but I tried my best to get through without choking up. I heard my mom suddenly scream and cry out, "No, no, NO!" and it sounded like she was running away from the phone. Then there was silence. I could hear my dad sniffling on the other end of the phone. I sat there, bowed my head with tears rolling down my face. My dad interrupted the silence with tears in his voice, "I am so sorry, Natalie, I am so sorry." He prayed and then we said goodbye.

10

The Beginning

I wiped the wetness from my face, gathered up my things, and slowly made my way to the hotel lobby. I could see out the windows and hear that it was raining. As bleary-eyed as I was, I remember thinking how fitting it was to have weather like this. The rain represented how I felt. I checked in, was given my room key and made my way to my room for the night.

As I was setting my things down in the room, I received a call from one of my department leaders. She told me how sorry she was that I wasn't able to make my flight and reassured me that, even though the earliest I could fly out of Zurich was the next afternoon, they were doing all they could to connect me with a chartered plane that would meet me in Toronto and take me directly to Kansas City. I cried when she told me this. I was beyond sad to have missed my flight, but to know that I would be getting home as quickly as possible was a relief.

She then said, "Natalie, I am so very sorry for your loss. I don't really know what else to say except that we are sending hugs from here in Kansas City and we are going to get you home as soon as possible. I know that you have a strong faith, and I hope that helps you now." I didn't know exactly what to say except what I felt: "I honestly don't know how it can get worse, but I have hope in God, that he's going to help us." I told her it meant a lot to me and then thanked her and hung up.

I managed to force myself to eat something and flipped on the TV to distract myself.

Intermittently my brain would wake up to reality and I would burst into tears. What had happened? How was this not a bad dream? What were we going to do now? In the midst of my jumbling thoughts and absolute shock, the only thing that kept racing through my mind like a searing knife was, *My eye . . . Oh God, my eye.*

Although it may be strange to read, in the Bible God calls Israel the apple of his eye and at that point I felt I could relate to his heart. Graham was the absolute apple of my eye, the very gift of God to my husband and me. I couldn't comprehend that a person I loved so much was just gone.

During one of these moments of being beside myself, I reached for my Bible. As a kid I often employed the "open to a random spot" strategy for my reading time. Not being able to think much at this point, I employed younger Natalie's strategy and opened my Bible to a random spot. It fell on Psalm 18, which I began to read aloud:

I love you, LORD, my strength.
    The LORD is my rock, my fortress and my deliverer;
my God is my rock, in whom I take refuge,
    my shield and the horn of my salvation, my stronghold.

I called to the LORD, who is worthy of praise,
    and I have been saved from my enemies.
The cords of death entangled me;
    the torrents of destruction overwhelmed me.
The cords of the grave coiled around me;
    the snares of death confronted me.

In my distress I called to the LORD;
    I cried to my God for help.
From his temple he heard my voice;
    my cry came before him, into his ears.
The earth trembled and quaked,
    and the foundations of the mountains shook;
they trembled because he was angry. (Psalm 18:1–7)

As soon as the words of verse 7 were leaving my mouth, I heard a literal clash of lighting and roll of thunder that startled me as I was sitting on the bed. Call it a coincidence or whatever you'd like, but in that moment I felt the Lord saying, "I see you and I hear you. I haven't left you alone." Tears flowing, I continued to read the rest of the chapter, which talked about God as a warrior and rescuer of his people.

This Psalm said what I needed to but didn't know how to put into words. I didn't need God to pat me on the head and say, "There, there my child." I needed a God who would fight for me and come to my rescue in my darkest hour—and this was it.

I tried to fall asleep, but my brain wouldn't shut off. The only thing that got me through the night was connecting to my church's streaming prayer service. It was 7:00 p.m. Thursday evening there; it was 2:00 a.m. in Zurich. Those minutes spent watching and praying along with them was the closest I came to relief. There was something so comforting about seeing familiar faces praising and praying and hearing the sounds of people who were sure of God. I was sure, too, but I needed to hear it from someone else. After watching for some time I was finally able to drift off for a couple of hours of fitful sleep.

Morning came and it was time to leave for home. I felt anticipation but also dread, knowing what awaited me there. I grabbed a handful of Kleenex that I knew I would need, threw back some ibuprofen, checked out of the hotel, and made my way to my gate. I don't remember much about my flight except trying to cover up my intermittent crying and attempting, with little success, to sleep.

I arrived in Toronto and found my driver. He took my luggage, put it in the back of the car, and shuttled me to the regional airport. I walked onto the tarmac and was greeted by two pilots who apparently knew the situation. "We are so sorry for your loss, Mrs. Weedman. We are going to get you home safely. We've even made up a bed for you so you can get some rest." I could have hugged them. I wanted to be home, but in the meantime, I wanted to sleep. I walked to the back of the jet and curled up with the blankets they laid out for me, put on an eye mask, and tried to turn my brain off.

We landed in Kansas City uneventfully, and I was safely shuttled home. As the car pulled away and I walked up to my front door, I knew that the version of Natalie who had walked out of that door only five days ago could never return. I took a deep breath and stepped inside.

The few days that followed were a blur. I don't remember much from that time except being surrounded by people and condolences, bouquets and cards. It was all hard to comprehend in the moment. By this time my parents and some of our extended family had gotten into town.

Thankfully, my amazing sister-in-law Torrie and dear friend Nichole had taken it upon themselves to bear the brunt of planning funeral arrangements on our behalf. The only question that remained was when to have the funeral itself. Unfortunately there really is no good time for a funeral, but this time was especially difficult. Graham had passed away on May 26. May 30 was Jesse's and my anniversary, and May 31 was my birthday. Jesse let me pick.

I chose May 31st.

Prior to the funeral, Jesse and I, along with our parents, went to see Graham at the funeral home. It's hard to describe the longing you have to see your child, even when his body is only an empty shell. But even that shell was so precious to me. As we approached the casket, I saw his beautiful profile. I noticed that even in the few days I had been gone he had grown! Tears started falling. I stroked his hair and kept whispering,

"I love you, buddy, I love you so much." Jesse and I stood there for several minutes taking it all in and crying.

During this time, my dad asked if he could pray for resurrection. We said yes! We knew God could do anything, and we came together in agreement to ask him. My dad began to pray, and we could feel the presence of the Lord come into the room so strongly. We prayed for several minutes, asking for Graham's spirit to return to his body. Even though he didn't wake up, we felt the reassuring presence of God surrounding and strengthening us.

Later that day I received a text message from my sister-in-law Courtney, who told us she had seen a vision. She knew from my parents-in-law that we had prayed for resurrection, but later that day the Lord showed her a picture of what was happening in heaven when we prayed. She said she saw Graham and a bunch of other kids in heaven running and playing and kicking a ball, and Jesus was standing with them nearby. She said as soon as the words began to be prayed, Jesus and Graham pulled a little away from the group and walked over to listen intently. She said that Jesus smiled, looked at Graham, and said, "Up to you." She said that Graham paused for a moment, but then grinned and turned to run off with his friends.

When she told me this I simultaneously laughed and teared up. Anyone who knew Graham knew that he loved any activity involving kicking or throwing, so that was completely characteristic of him. We knew that God heard our prayer, but to see it play out through that picture was a moment we will never forget.

Two days later the funeral took place. We stood at the front of the reception room as friends, family, and colleagues lined up to give their condolences and hugs. We had chosen an open casket for Graham. I remember placing all kinds of keepsakes in the casket with him: a baseball glove we had bought him before he was born, a baseball bat signed by everyone who came to his first birthday party, a little puppet bear he loved. We also put Graham in our favorite lion pajamas. Maybe it's just a mom thing, but getting Graham ready for bed was one of my favorite tasks because it was when he was at his cleanest and cutest. We would give him a bath, get him dressed for bed, then put some good smelling product in his hair and comb it over like an old man. The PJs were a little form fitting, and I remember his little belly and diaper bum would stick out. It was the cutest!

It came time for the service to start. It felt like a church service. Almost everyone who was involved in administrating, other than the funeral home staff, were from our faith community—people who donated their time out of love for us. Even our former worship pastor had flown in from Nashville to lead worship specially for the funeral, bringing with him two songs he had written for us. After worship, we sat down for a few words from our pastor and then the slideshow of our favorite photos and videos of Graham.

The last video in the slideshow was one that I had taken the day I left for Zurich. Even in grief it was such a good feeling for other people to see his funny personality and laugh along with us. Several of our family members got up to speak, including my dad, my father-in-law, and my brothers-in-law. Even in the sorrow of the moment, their words were touching and powerful.

Finally Jesse and I went up to the podium to say a few words. I read Graham one last bedtime story, his favorite: *The Going to Bed Book* by Sandra Boynton. Then Jesse took the microphone and told everyone he wanted to do one thing: say one last blessing over Graham. This was his heart. It was his nature as a father. A man who spoke a blessing over his son every day was now speaking one over him as he laid him to rest.

The service wrapped up and we made our way to the gravesite. A few days earlier, Jesse and I had combed the cemetery for the perfect spot. We knew we wanted a plot with a lot of space and under a tree. Even from the time he was itty-bitty, Graham liked his personal space. He would only put up with cuddling for so long before he would try to squirm away. Although sometimes right before bed he would be so sleepy that we could sneak in a few more cuddles than usual. The spot was perfect because of its location under a beautiful flowering tree. Often during our rides in the car or going on a walk, we would notice Graham getting quiet and staring up at the trees. It didn't matter if there were leaves or not, he loved them! Thankfully due to the generosity of our colleagues and friends who set up an online donation page for funeral expenses, we were also able to purchase two additional plots—one on either side of Graham—to ensure the space he loved so much remained until Jesse and I could join him.

We all arrived at his plot where we sang another song, and our pastor spoke a few more words. Then one final prayer wrapped up the service. Most of our friends meandered back to their cars, but Jesse and I and a few others lingered a little longer. This was the last time our eyes would see the casket that held our son.

Jesse and I said our final goodbyes and walked into our new lives as bereaved parents.

Chapter 2

A Theme in the Aftermath

W hen you become a parent, you are constantly aware of where your child is and feel a weight of responsibility for them that is precious and makes you constantly alert. There was more than one time that Jesse and I both woke up in the weeks following the funeral, startled because we hadn't heard Graham wake up yet, only to remember his room was empty. It was awful.

Thankfully our employer told us to take all the time off we needed, so we ended up spending an additional four weeks at home, taking grief as it came and adjusting to our new normal. In the hustle and bustle of funeral and family activities, Jesse and I hadn't had a chance to talk about what had happened in the days leading up to Graham's passing. We still did not know what had gone wrong with Graham. However, we hoped the autopsy would provide us with some answers. During this time at home, Jesse and I sat down together and he told me about those last days.

Jesse told me that Graham, who had been hesitant to walk before I left, although he knew how, had been walking all over the house like a rock star. Jesse also said that Graham kept looking for me. Even a noise in another part of the house would prompt him to go over and investigate to see if I had come home. My momma heart exploded when he told me that. Graham had actually noticed I was gone!

Then we started to talk about the night before his death. Had anything seemed different? Did Graham seem like himself? Jesse said everything seemed normal, in fact they had gone out for fast food that night to get out of the house and get Graham one of his favorite foods, French fries. The nighttime routine had gone as expected. Although this didn't give any clues as to what had happened, it made me so happy to know that Graham's last night on earth was uneventful and full of fried food!

About eight weeks after the funeral, we finally got the call that the results had come in. We immediately got in the car and made our way over to the funeral home. Driving the same tree-lined roads we had the day of his funeral, I remember telling Jesse about how relieved I was that we would finally have some answers and some closure.

When we arrived at the funeral home, we met with the director, who took us back to a room to present the certificate. He gave us some privacy to look it over. We quickly scanned the document to find the cause of death. We did not expect what it said: CAUSE UNKNOWN. We flipped through the pages again, each one containing information about his every organ and system—all noted as completely perfect. We sat there in shock silence, staring at the paperwork, not knowing what to say. On one hand, we felt relief. We hadn't missed something. There wasn't anything that could have warned us what was ahead. On the other hand, not having an apparent reason made it feel all the more senseless. Technically it couldn't even be called SIDS since he was over a year old. What do you even do with, "Our son passed away, but we have no idea why"? Instead of fewer unknowns, we had more.

When I spoke to Jesse on the phone in Zurich, something that had come out of my mouth almost intuitively was, "We don't know what to do, but our eyes are on you, Lord." After receiving the autopsy report, those words came to our lips again. At the time, I didn't remember where it was from in the Bible, but I later looked it up. That very phrase was spoken by the Israelite King Jehoshaphat in 2 Chronicles 20. He was a king who followed in the ways of the Lord and one whom God blessed. It says, "After this, the Moabites and Ammonites with some of the Meunites came to wage war against Jehoshaphat" (v. 1). In his alarm, Jehoshaphat resolved to inquire of the Lord and brought Judah together to seek the Lord at the temple. While at the temple, Jehoshaphat began to pray aloud:

> "Lord, the God of our ancestors, are you not the God who is in heaven? You rule over all the kingdoms of the nations. Power and might are in your hand, and no one can withstand you. Our God, did you not drive out the inhabitants of this land before your people Israel and give it forever to the descendants of Abraham your friend? They have lived in it and have built in it a sanctuary for your Name, saying, 'If calamity comes upon us, whether the sword of judgment, or plague or famine, we will stand in your presence before this temple that bears your Name and will cry out to you in our distress, and you will hear us and save us.'
>
> "But now here are men from Ammon, Moab and Mount Seir, whose territory you would not allow Israel to invade when they came from Egypt; so they turned away from them and did not destroy them. See how they are repaying us by coming to drive us out of the possession you gave us as an inheritance. Our God, will you not judge them? For we have no power to face this vast army that is attacking us. We do not know what to do, but our eyes are on you." (2 Chron. 20:6–12)

Prior to this Judah had lived in prosperity and peace. Second Chronicles even says that Israel's mortal enemies, the Philistines, had brought Jehoshaphat tribute at the start of his reign.

Now out of nowhere, there stood a vast army seemingly ready to take them out at any moment. What strikes me immediately is that Jehoshaphat did not say, "Why, oh, why, God is this happening to us? We did everything right! We are righteous! We are following your law! This doesn't make sense." Nor did he overanalyze circumstances or try to dissect his or Israel's behavior. Jehoshaphat instead went immediately to the Lord, recognizing where God had brought Israel from and how he had helped them in the past. He made it clear they were running to him and asking him to help them. Then he recognized that they had no power within themselves to face down the enemy. The cherry on top was then, He ended his prayer with "We don't know what to do but our eyes are on you, Lord."

Some of you may know how this ends in 2 Chronicles. The prophet Jahaziel prophesies to King Jehoshaphat and tells him, "The battle is not yours, but God's... You will not have to fight this battle...Stand firm and see the deliverance the Lord will give you" (2 Chron. 20:15–17). The next day Israel went out to face their enemies with the praisers leading the way. Verse 22 tells us that as they began to sing and praise, the Lord set ambushes for their enemies. They destroyed each other before the Israelites could even get close to them!

"We don't know what to do, but our eyes are on you," became a sort of context for how Jesse and I began to process grief. We made that our theme. It was something that came out of us in our prayers, our discussions with others, and sometimes even in social media posts. We decided not to "know" anything else besides that. Like Jehoshaphat we felt very strongly that we needed to focus on what was ahead of us and not get dragged down into "why's." As we sought to focus on the Lord in the midst of the battle, we gave him the space to fight for us.

In the aftermath of your loved one's passing, I encourage you to ask the Lord what the theme is for you and your family. Maybe something has already been resonating in your heart, but you dismissed it as random. Or perhaps you feel that "We don't know what to do but our eyes are on you" applies for you as well. Whether it is a particular Scripture, a music lyric or an encouraging phrase that you hear over and over again in your heart, pay attention and write it down.

As we seek the Lord in the face of the battle, the Holy Spirit is so kind to give us something to hold on to.

Questions to Ponder

1. Like King Jehoshaphat, what unknowns are you facing in your grief journey?

2. What theme do you feel like the Holy Spirit is giving you after loss?

A Prayer in the Processing

Father, I thank you that I can call on your name when I need help. Your name is high above every other name. No one compares to you! I thank you that you have always been good to me. I look back and remember how you've helped me through [specifics]. I have seen your blessing and favor in my life.

Now Lord, I am bringing these circumstances and this heartache to you. I don't know what to do about it and I need your help. Please don't delay when I call to you! Hear me, Lord, and answer me quickly. You said that you would be close to the brokenhearted, that you would rescue me when I call to you. I am asking you to do that for me. I thank you that I can rely on you in every season. I look to you alone.

In Jesus's name, amen.

Chapter 3

Grieve, Wash, and Repeat

B efore experiencing loss myself, I really did not have any preconceived ideas of what grief would look like. Being thrown into it after Graham passed and with the added finality of the autopsy report, I struggled to find my footing in a new normal but also my relationship with the Lord. It was a strange time.

There was a very real question of, "What do I do now, God?" In the process of becoming a parent, it becomes your identity—it's who you are. What happens when that part of you just stops?

There were many times of extreme heaviness, sadness, and turmoil that were emotionally and physically overwhelming. Sometimes Jesse and I would find solace in talking it out, crying it out, or remembering some of our favorite moments with Graham. Sometimes I would look at photos or watch videos to feel close to Graham. Mostly, though, I felt driven to a quiet place to be with the Lord, usually Graham's room. This is where I would absolutely unload every emotion, every sob, every tear before the Lord. I would lay on the floor next to Graham's crib with a box of tissues and my Bible next to me. I would pray, cry, weep, and wail. I would tell the Lord how much I missed my son, how much it hurt, how I didn't understand, how I hated how I felt, how much I needed his help.

There were other times that I couldn't do anything except put my face in a pillow and cry out to God in deep anguish. It was not uncommon for me to give myself migraines because of the force of emotion and strain that would come out in those times with the Lord.

After the torrent of emotions came out, I would feel spent. Then I would lay there in stillness and just listen. At that point I was too tired to do anything else. Amazingly, I would feel the presence of God wash over me. In those moments I truly feel like my spiritual ears opened and I would hear his voice. Often he would remind me that he saw me, that he still had a plan, that he hadn't forgotten us, that he still had a promise on our lives.

"Grieve, wash, repeat" became sort of a pattern for me as I walked out my grief journey day by day. I would feel a build up, then there would be release and the Holy Spirit would wash over me right after. What struck me about it is that God came to me with such gentleness and kindness in those still moments. It might sound trite due to the limitations of the English language, but it was one of the first times I had experienced that side of his nature so personally. It wasn't gentleness and kindness in the benevolent, general sense, it was specific and personal. I felt it directed at me, pointedly. I could feel him so close to me, surrounding me, speaking kind words to me. It felt as safe and comforting as an embrace.

This feeling was familiar to me, but only recently. The only other time I had experienced that so personally was actually a week before Graham passed. Our church customarily held services on Friday evenings, which we would usually attend as a family. This time however I had gone by myself. Graham had been feeling a little under the weather, so dad kept him home to get him to bed at a decent time. This particular Friday, one of our senior pastors was speaking about Acts 20:24, "But my life is worth nothing to me unless I use it for finishing the work assigned me by the Lord Jesus—the work of telling others the Good News about the wonderful grace of God" (NLT). At the end of the service there was a moment where many in the congregation, including myself, responded by coming up to the altar and kneeling, many crying. Even our pastor was crying and kneeling at the front. It was a holy moment, full of reverential awe and wonder. As we knelt there, we each prayed words of dedication to the Lord. I was personally overcome, feeling the tangible and weighty presence of the Lord. It was not unfamiliar to me, but this time it felt different. I felt an overwhelming tenderness and a gentleness coming from God that I had never experienced before. In that moment it was almost as if he was pulling me in close, like a father would pull his child in for an embrace in a special moment. It was precious, and even now as I'm writing these words I can't do it except through tears. A friend who watched a recording of the service weeks later actually sent the clip of that moment to me and remarked how special it was. Looking back, it was preparation for what I didn't know was ahead.

One of the things I wanted to accomplish with this book was to be very real about how I processed grief—to honestly share things I actually did and said. If you don't think I'm crazy for screaming into pillows and giving full vent to my emotions by pounding the carpet, hold on to your hat. Seriously though, there were so many ways that God ministered to me when I decided I was going to take the limits off what I thought I should do. I kept the word of God as my foundation and asked the Holy Spirit to help me as I walked through grief, and I found that he did, in very creative ways!

One of those ways was a feeling of extra sensitivity to the presence of the Lord and, somewhat surprisingly to me, angels. For whatever reason,

I had never thought much about angels and their ministry to believers prior to that. But after Graham died, I would often feel the presence of angels in our house. Many times I would sense them during prayer, but I would also sense them when Jesse and I were sitting in our living room talking to other people. In the weeks and months following our loss, we would have friends and family visit. During that time the conversation would inevitably turn to Graham and how we were doing. Even in the middle of our hurt and processing, and honestly not knowing what to say except that we were trusting in the Lord, I would feel the presence of God in the room and with him the presence of angelic beings. There were times I could even tell where they were in the room. It felt as though they were listening into our conversation with interest, and peculiarly, with delight. Often the Scripture that came to mind during those times was Malachi 3:16, "Then those who feared the LORD talked with each other, and the LORD listened and heard. A scroll of remembrance was written in his presence concerning those who feared the LORD and honored his name." We felt as though our words were being heard and marked.

After a few times of this happening, God revealed to me that some of these ministering spirits were Graham's angels. Hebrews 1:14 says, "Are not all angels ministering spirits sent to serve those who will inherit salvation?" In the next moment God began to address something I could barely bring myself to think about: Graham's last moments. Not knowing exactly what happened to Graham, we didn't know if he was gone in an instant or in minutes. The thought of my child suffering was something I could not even comprehend. However in that revelation I felt God confirm in my spirit that Graham had passed in an instant. In fact, God revealed to me that it was Graham's angel who had "woken him up" on the other side the night that he passed. The Lord impressed so firmly on my heart that even though Graham may have been physically alone in his room, he was surrounded by protection, by comfort, even by familiarity. Out of all the ways the Lord ministered to me through the years, this remains one of the most precious.

I never walked in with any preconceived notion of what was going to happen in my personal time with the Lord. I simply responded from my heart and poured it out to the Lord, and then gave him space to respond to me in turn. Honestly it was probably the first time in my life that my hands were completely off the steering wheel, and I knew what it felt like to fully trust the Lord with all my heart, with all my grief, and with every part of my soul. But really when you think about it, that is what a healthy relationship is all about. Using marriage as an example, I know there are some things I just don't have to worry about because Jesse is going to take care of it. God is the same. He is trustworthy. Do we trust him to take us through the dark places of grief and hurt without feeling like we have to control the experience or that we have to guard against going too far?

Questions to Ponder

1. How has God been calling you to draw closer to him in the middle of your grief?

2. Do you feel like you have any hang-ups in your relationship with God that prevent you from going to that place with him?

3. Have you talked to God about those hang-ups?

I wanted to ask those questions specifically because one of the things I struggled with for many years (even prior to grief) was feeling like there was some insufficiency in my own ability to connect with God. I was too in my head about it. I didn't like awkward silences. I didn't know how to get more deeply connected in the Spirit.

Don't get me wrong, I would still pray and get something out of it, but there were sort of these underlying frustrations with my own ability to go to a deeper place. But at a certain point I realized that I was trying to figure it out on my own *(How do I do this? How can I make this better?)* but I wasn't going to God about it. It's almost like feeling the need to clean myself up a little before approaching him.

I decided instead of doing all that processing in my head, I needed to make that part of my conversation with God. I would often tell him, "Lord, I don't know how to do this very well, but I love you and I want to connect with you. Will you help me with that? Will you fill me? Will you make me more like you? Will you help me, Lord?" Then I would declare his character and who he is, sometimes even speaking out some psalms out loud. Before I knew it, I would feel his presence sweeping over me and filling me up.

Think about it: Is there any parent you know of that wouldn't absolutely do what their child is asking them to do when they come to them with a heart desiring connection like that? Realizing I could take even my most basic questions about connection to him was in and of itself establishing connection!

As I mentioned earlier, those same questions popped up again postloss. The truth is I didn't know what to do, but by that time I had established a pattern with God that I was going to come to him with my most basic self. I was going to come to him like a child, without feeling like

I needed to rationalize my feelings, or try to get over guilty feelings, or to pep talk myself through disconnection. I just needed him. And I told him so! He was safe. And I told him so! He was truth. And I told him so! He said he was going to help me. And I told him so. When I approached him like that, I felt how much joy he had in helping me and in showing me his nature.

A Prayer in the Processing

Lord, I come to you with all my heart. How I need you! I don't know what to do with these emotions, with this hurt, with this pain. Would you help me, Lord? Would you be near as I seek you and reach out to you with all my heart? I take the limits off my time with you. I want you to minister to me as you see fit. I trust you completely, knowing that you are close to the brokenhearted and you won't forsake those who seek you. I look to you, I trust in you, and I ask Lord that you would do what I can't. My eyes are on you, Lord. You are the only one who can help me. Fill me and help me lean into you more fully.

In Jesus's name, amen.

Chapter 4

Entering the Wrestle

Prayer does not equip us for greater works. Prayer is the greater work. Prayer is the working of the miracles of redemption in me, which produces the miracle of redemption in others through the power of God.[2]

—Oswald Chambers, *My Utmost for His Highest*

Many of us know the account of Abraham's grandson Jacob in the Bible. He was the younger twin brother of a man named Esau. The Bible says that even before they were born his mother, Rebecca, could feel them wrestling in her womb. Obviously wondering what was going on, the Lord told her there were two nations within her and that "the older will serve the younger" (Gen. 25:23). Even from birth, there was a promise on Jacob's life.

As the boys grew older, it became apparent that Jacob did not plan to just wait around for those words to come to pass. In those days the rights of the firstborn were encapsulated in two areas: the birthright and the blessing. The birthright had to do with the inheritance and position in the family to be recognized as the leader, and the blessing was a special prophecy about the future that was irrevocable. Jacob slyly enticed Esau to trade his birthright for a bowl of stew and then outright stole (with the help of his mother) Esau's blessing by lying about his identity to his blind father. As you would guess, Esau was not too pleased when he realized what Jacob had done, so he made plans to kill him. Discovering this, Rebecca sent Jacob away to her extended family in another land. On the way there, the Bible says that Jacob had a dream and saw a stairway to heaven. He saw the Lord, who confirmed his promise to Jacob to give him the land and make him a great nation. When Jacob arrived in Rebecca's homeland, he found their relative Laban and married his two daughters. Over many years he was blessed with a large family and huge flocks.

At a certain time, the Lord told Jacob it was time to go back home. Knowing he did not leave Esau on the best terms, Jacob decided to send some gifts ahead of his entourage to announce his arrival and hopefully soften any anger that had lingered over the years.

However, after Jacob did this, he heard from his men that Esau was coming to meet them with thousands of men. Yikes! Like many of us would do, Jacob panicked. The Bible says in Genesis 32:7–8:

> In great fear and distress Jacob divided the people who were with him into two groups, and the flocks and herds and camels as well. He thought, "If Esau comes and attacks one group, the group that is left may escape."

In a somewhat surprising move, Jacob sends the two groups across the river while he himself stayed behind and spends the night in the camp. Genesis 32:24 says: "So Jacob was left alone, and a man wrestled with him till daybreak."

Probably a million times, I have glazed over that verse. Maybe you have too. But think about the oddness of that for a moment. Esau was across the river waiting for him. Jacob's family was split up and in fear of their lives. Jacob found himself completely alone, in fear and distress. Then in the middle of this, God pulls Jacob into a wrestling match. I don't know about you, but considering the circumstances and what Jacob was facing it seemed like a strange proposition and even stranger timing.

The Bible tells us the rest of the story:

> When the man saw that he could not overpower him, he touched the socket of Jacob's hip so that his hip was wrenched as he wrestled with the man. Then the man said, "Let me go, for it is daybreak."
>
> But Jacob replied, "I will not let you go unless you bless me." The man asked him, "What is your name?" "
>
> Jacob," he answered.
>
> Then the man said, "Your name will no longer be Jacob, but Israel, because you have struggled with God and with humans and have overcome." (Gen. 32:25–28)

Surprisingly it seems Jacob was actually the one prolonging this struggle. You would think it would be the other way around! I can almost hear him saying to himself, *Oh yeah? You started this, but I'm going to end it.* The man even tried to wrench Jacob's hip in an effort to get away. However, at some point Jacob realized this wasn't about Esau across the river, his family, or even his personal safety. This was about something else entirely.

At the beginning of the passage, the Bible says Jacob was completely alone. There is a parallel to our grief journey here. Of course, we hope to be surrounded by loving and supportive people who understand, as it says in Romans 12:15, to "mourn with those who mourn."

However, even with wonderful people around you, there will be times when, like Jacob, you will find yourself completely and utterly alone. It could be a physical isolation like Jacob, or the realization that there are just certain points of your grief process that can't be fully understood by someone else—even a spouse or close loved one. It can't be distracted or medicated away. It must be dealt with between you and the Lord. But like Jacob, we have to realize it's about more than just grief. There is something else at play here.

This is exactly where I found myself after Graham passed, but it took me years to recognize it and put words to it—even as I was in the middle of it. There was something about my grief processing that didn't quite make sense, even to me. I felt God engaging my heart in new ways, inviting me to push past what I had known. There was this urge to grapple, to wrestle out my grief in the presence of God. I could, of course, tie this to the loss of my son, but I knew it wasn't just about grief. Like Jacob, I knew I needed to fully engage and see it through to the end, even though I couldn't wrap my brain around it entirely. Talk about me being out of my element!

I believe for some of you this is a diagnosis for where you are right now. Like me, you can feel the Lord pulling on your heart and calling you to a place to get away with him and wrestle some things out. Maybe you're battling your own mind because you feel like it doesn't make sense. After all, this is about grief, isn't it? Maybe you've even thought, *I'm going crazy!* Perhaps you feel limited by what is "allowed" in your wrestle. You may feel that, if you allow yourself to go to that place, you don't know what will happen.

Let me encourage you to take the limits off! If God can handle Jacob's not letting go of him, even going so far as to wrench Jacob's hip, I would venture to say that he can handle your hurt, your sorrow, your anger, your questions...your everything! This is not some tame wrestle. This is a knock-down, drag-out fight that changes you. It's meant to be.

Maybe the reason why it's so confusing is that we are used to the context of the Lord taking our weaknesses and our imperfections and creating strength. After all, it's biblical right? But sometimes we don't realize when God is trying to get us to a place of emptiness and transformation, like he did with Jacob. Your strength is required for the wrestle, but it's not the end result. We're supposed to leave it all on the mat. Remember Jacob walked out of the wrestle with a limp that he had for the rest of his life. He could've said, "Lord, don't you know what I'm facing? How am I supposed to run away from Esau now? Thanks a lot!" Had he been distracted by his current circumstances or unsure of God's intention, he would've missed out on what God was trying to accomplish. It's the same with us.

In the thick of my wrestle with the Lord, I would often go to Graham's room to read the Bible and pray, but there were other times when I would go on drives through the backroads near our house. Since Jesse and I lived in the middle unit of a fourplex at the time, it was really the only place that I felt I could be as loud as I wanted. Believe me when I say I let it all out in those moments, without reservation. I would cry, pound my steering wheel, tell the Lord I needed his help. Often it felt like I was pushing on invisible constraints that wanted to keep me locked up and weighed down, unable to really connect with the Lord and get the help I needed. I told him I hated how that felt. I hated how I felt as a mom who no longer had her kid. I laid my whole soul bare. In those moments I didn't think, *Wow, I am doing such a great job with this wrestling thing. Gosh, God is going to bless me so much.* Beyond the relief of spilling out my emotions, it didn't make me feel stronger or more confident in myself. Like Jacob, I fully felt that limp. But as I would begin to declare God's promises in that same breath, I felt I was grabbing more fully onto the Lord. I wasn't going to let go until he blessed me.

Yes, the wrestle may leave us feeling weaker in ourselves, but remember that a limp was not the only thing Jacob walked away with. As daylight broke, the man told Jacob to let him go. Jacob refused to do so unless the man blessed him. I don't know about you, but when I hear blessing, my mind automatically jumps to the benefits of serving the Lord as outlined in Deuteronomy 28. In this context, however, blessedness took on a new form. Jacob got a name change! He went from "someone who grasps at man's heal," to "someone who wrestled with God and overcame." I believe that in that moment, Jacob, now Israel, truly walked into his destiny as the father of nations. Before it had been a promise combined with his own "grasping" (his human effort and conniving), but after this wrestling match it was about walking in a new blessedness—a new identity that was not obtained through human effort but bestowed by God himself.

Friends, God has our circumstances fully in mind. He knows the turmoil, the pain, and everything else going on inside of you. He cares about you. However, we also need to understand when there is more at play than just the obvious. Circumstances may be what they are, but we have to understand what God is after in the middle of them. He is inviting us to a new place, full of meaning and fruitfulness—if we don't get confused by the feeling of being pulled into the wrestle. Long before Israel was known as a great nation, he was first known as the man who wrestled with God. The message for us today is this: God is calling all of us into a deeper place, a place of great vulnerability and blessing. One that marks and changes us just as it did Jacob. On the other side of that wrestle is a new name and a reaffirmed future. Even if it feels awkward and unknown, I encourage you to say yes.

Maybe, for you, saying yes to the wrestle is about being vulnerable and open about what you're thinking and feeling without trying to clean it up first. Maybe it's lamenting to him that you don't really know how to do this "right." Maybe it's being honest about your feelings of disconnection or your concerns about the aftermath in your family. Maybe it's fully leaning into the reality of your circumstances but still declaring his promise.

At different times for me it was all of those things! The point is to come to him with our most basic selves, with all the baggage and feelings that go with that, and throw them all into the wrestle. Then, like Jacob, don't let go! As those who say yes to the wrestle, we can be confident in God's character, knowing he only has our best interest at heart. As we wrestle it out with him, we will find his promise for us going so much further beyond earthly blessing to transform us in creative ways.

What I find amazing about how this story ultimately ends is that even though God's intention for Jacob was fulfilled in the wrestle, he didn't just ignore Jacob's current circumstances. We find that while Jacob's attention was being consumed by the wrestle, God softened Esau's heart, diffusing the circumstance that concerned Jacob most. Whether it happened that night or earlier, we don't know. But the Bible says that when Esau saw Jacob, he "ran to meet Jacob and embraced him; he threw his arms around his neck and kissed him. And they wept" (Gen. 33:4).

What that means for each of us in our individual grief journeys is really open to God's creative interpretation and our participation. Unfortunately, grief doesn't just go away, but we can be sure to receive something in the wrestling exchange that transforms and equips us to face anything. The details may look different for each person and their grief journey, but be sure that God's purpose is always the same.

Questions to Ponder

1. Can you identify aspects of your grief journey that may actually be God calling you into a spiritual wrestle?

2. Has there been anything preventing you from engaging with God in this way?

3. How is God calling you to be more real with him as you process grief?

A Prayer in the Processing

Lord, I say yes to wrestling out my grief and trauma with you. I don't understand everything, and I don't know everything. But just like Jacob, I am determined to throw my whole self into the wrestle and not let go! Help me to grasp more firmly on to you when circumstances and emotions feel overwhelming. I know that your intention is to transform and equip me for whatever I face. Thank you for helping me. Thank you for caring enough to wrestle this out with me.

In Jesus's name, amen.

Chapter 5

Breaking Before the Lord

⌒

Then I heard a loud voice in heaven say:
"Now have come the salvation and the power
and the kingdom of our God,
and the authority of his Messiah.
For the accuser of our brothers and sisters,
who accuses them before our God day and night,
has been hurled down."

—Revelation 12:10

The Bible says that Satan is an accuser of the saints and that he used to stand before the Lord making his accusations day and night. Unfortunately, he had that right when Adam and Eve sinned in the Garden. Also unfortunately, the unredeemed humans who came after Adam and Eve certainly supplied him with a lot of accusation material. However, when Jesus died for our sins and rose to his position in heaven, Satan was "hurled down," away from the throne of God, and now apparently in our earthly backyard.

I very rarely hear anyone talk about the voices we hear in general, but especially in grief. Depending on your level of awareness and the type of biblical teaching you have had, you may not realize how the enemy uses accusing voices as a key tool to undermine our grief journey.

Turns out the accuser is still the accuser; he is just in a new arena.

Even after Jesse and I received the autopsy report, I heard ridiculous thoughts in my head: "I'll bet it happened because you started giving him dairy the month before. Or maybe it was that slip and fall in the kitchen two weeks prior. What about that ear infection medication the doctor gave him? Maybe it was a bad batch." Or even, "I'll bet the autopsy report is wrong. I bet I did miss something." It didn't come in some weird slithery voice; it sounded like my own! For me, there were three things at play here:

1. Very real grief

2. A very natural human desire for certainty

3. A very real enemy who wants to bring destruction into our lives and will try to throw any falsehood or half-truth to get us to open the door to it

The Bible tells us that the devil is an accuser and like a lion that seeks to devour. I have watched enough of the National Geographic channel to know that predators will target those of the pack that they perceive to be the weakest. Unfortunately, grief makes us a spiritual target. In the midst of one of the greatest fights of your life, you better know the enemy will try to take full advantage. He will throw up every memory; he will bring to recollection anything you could have possibly missed or opportunities you did not take that could have changed the outcome. He knows that it's human nature to seek certainty (even if it is unpleasant), and he would love nothing more than to serve you up a steaming hot pile of his lies and get you to agree with them. Or even make you think those thoughts are your own! It doesn't matter how outlandish they are.

Sometimes I would not realize what was happening until I had been ruminating on thoughts for half a day, becoming more depressed and hopeless with each passing hour. For me it always started off as a memory that would lead to thoughts about "maybe that's what happened," and then I would think of something else . . . and something else. At some point I would wake up to what was happening, realizing, like a kid who had inadvertently wandered into a dark alley, I was in a place I did not belong. For Jesse, you can imagine it was even more difficult since he was the only one home when Graham passed. We had to work at guarding our minds, and it was a fight.

Jesse and I weren't the only ones who heard these voices. At different times we would talk to family members who would say in amazement, "Oh my gosh, I have heard those voices too." Even family members who had seen him only a handful of times while he was alive would say this, which objectively is ridiculous (and we know that). Just know that no matter the circumstances of your loved one's passing, the enemy is ruthless and will likely try to talk to you about how you played a role or missed an opportunity. If you feel that you could have made a mistake or missed an opportunity leading up to the loss of your loved one, like neglecting to say I love you or not making up for an argument, it's so important to stop in your tracks as soon as you become aware of it and bring it immediately to the Lord. Don't entertain any thoughts planted by the enemy, no matter how "true" you think they might be!

After Graham's passing, we were connected to many people who had also experienced the loss of a child. There was a couple I remember who had lost their young child to an accident at home. I don't know the exact circumstances, but from what I could tell, they blamed themselves (or each other). Something had been missed, and it led to a tragic outcome. I have often thought about that couple and prayed for them, my heart breaking for them. It's one thing to lose a child, but to also feel like somehow you were responsible is a tough road.

So when it comes to accusing voices, what do you do when you start to believe them? I will never forget one day I was talking to Jesse because I was processing some of the stuff I had been hearing. He said something very simple but profound: "Even if it was 100 percent true, it changes nothing. It just makes you feel more despair and hopelessness in the aftermath. It only maximizes death." This was a mini revelation to me. Even if this lie was 100 percent true, the enemy actually has no right to speak to you about it, period. The kindness and truth of the Lord sets us free, gives us hope, and restores us, even in the most tragic circumstances or in the aftermath of regret.

If we accept the "truth" from the enemy, we will sink more deeply into a despair that we feel is our justified burden to bear. One of my school of ministry teachers would say, "We break before the Lord, we do not break before the enemy." That is so good and so relevant in this context. The enemy wants us to break before our circumstances, break before accusing voices, break before his "truth." He loves it even more if he can whip us into such a frenzy that we turn on the people around us with his accusing voice. Don't let your mind entertain any voices that are designed to trap you and bring more destruction. Bring the truth of your circumstances to the Lord. Refuse to engage with voices that push you into despair or hopelessness. They have no place in your life. Be determined to submit every thought to the Lord through the power of the Holy Spirit. If you feel like you're breaking, do it before the Lord!

When I think about mistakes, I think about King David. This was a guy who made a few rather large mistakes. In 2 Samuel, he was confronted by the prophet Nathan. David repented, but the thing that strikes me is that he did not wallow in guilt and despair. What did he do instead? Psalm 51 shows us. He poured out his repentance, his lament, his praise, his heart to the Lord. Even more than that, he said, "Against you (Lord), you only, have I sinned" (Ps. 51:4). I'll be honest, there is something of human justice that doesn't seem quite right in that statement. What about the family of the man he killed? But at the end of the day, David was right. The life he took ultimately belonged to the Lord.

That is what I would consider breaking before God, not your enemy. David could have very easily retreated into himself, taken what he thought he deserved, been consumed by voices of guilt and destruction. Although he knew he deserved judgement, he didn't self-destruct, as the enemy would have loved for him to do. Instead he humbled himself and threw himself on the mercy of the Lord. In Psalm 51:17, he wrote, "My sacrifice, O God, is a broken spirit; a broken and contrite heart you, God, will not despise." What is amazing to me is that, despite his mistakes and the natural ramifications of his actions, God called him a man after his own heart.

Other lies you hear may be about your future. Have you heard voices saying it's inevitable that your family will be broken up because of a tragic loss? Or that you and your spouse will probably drift apart because your child is gone? Maybe it's about your own ability to cope. *I've never been any good under stress, and now this? I'll probably be numbing myself for the rest of my life.* No matter if it's those words exactly or something like that, learn to recognize when the enemy is working you. He wants you to accept his voice as your own thoughts, and he wants his words to come out of your mouth. He wants you to act on those thoughts. His goal in any tragedy is maximum destruction, so he will try to make destruction spread as far as possible.

As believers we need to be aware and vigilant when it comes to examining our thoughts against the truth of God's Word and to recognize when we are being targeted by a hungry lion.

I would like to say that, after I realized the enemy was speaking to me the first time, I never had any issues with it again. But every so often I would find myself subconsciously retracing a familiar path of thoughts that led me deeper and deeper into a brooding state of dread and despair. As soon as I realized it, I would immediately go to the Lord. I would quite literally tattle on the enemy. For me this wasn't just an internal process; it wasn't just about trying to think better thoughts. *(Does that work for anyone?)* It was about redirecting everything within me to the Lord, which meant making words come out of my mouth.

I would go into Graham's room, read Scriptures out loud, and declare that I was submitting every thought to the Lord. Sometimes I would even sing the psalms, declaring God's goodness just as David did. I didn't care what it looked or sounded like, or even if the verse directly related to grief. As truth was declared and the name of the Lord was lifted high, I knew every lie had to flee.

Sometimes it took a while for my feelings to catch up, but I decided that if the enemy was going to whisper lies, then I wasn't going to be afraid to "shout" the truth. The truth about God, the truth about myself, the truth from his Word. It was amazing that as I did this, the enemy figured out that he couldn't just throw his trash in my mind without repercussions, and eventually this stopped.

It wasn't about saying a certain prayer a certain way; it was about refusing to give the enemy any ground and constantly redirecting my attention to the one who could help me. I would speak from my heart, declare God's Word, and give full vent to my emotions during those times. And I was determined to keep doing that as many times as was necessary.

I think it's really important to mention that some of these battles are not won by yourself. You need the Holy Spirit, but you also need other people in your life who can speak truth. It may be a relative, a close friend, a pastor, a counselor, or a therapist. Whatever you do, seek out good counsel from people who are mature in the Lord and filled with the Holy Spirit. I can't tell you how many conversations I've had where, in telling a trusted person what I've been struggling with, they were able to speak truth and faith into my situation and bring clarity and relief. It was also not uncommon for them to prophetically speak to other things I'd been dealing with in the process. This is just one of the ways God ministered creatively to me.

Let me perhaps state the obvious here, but there are natural feelings of grief that come with loss that we must experience in our processing. There is no way around it, only through. That's where God wants to help us. Then there is the enemy, who is an opportunist and who would like to take those natural feelings and turn them into something destructive in your and your family's lives. I want to stress that unpleasant thoughts are a natural part of your grief journey, but you must realize what you're dealing with in any given moment. Not all unpleasant emotions come from the enemy, but you must recognize when those unpleasant emotions are a result of the enemy planting lies or trying to antagonize you.

You mustn't simply put on a happy face, but you do need to reject the lies that the enemy would like to tell you in the midst of strong emotions. Ask the Lord for wisdom to know what you're dealing with, and he will show you! Like a car shifts gears, it's very easy for me now to tell when I'm in the wrong gear. I rarely get very far in my thinking before I realize something is off. This is how it will be for you as well. The more we redirect our attention to the God of all truth, the less power any lie has over us.

Questions to Ponder

1. Can you identify thoughts the enemy has been planting to bring hopelessness and despair into your life?

2. What is the truth from God's Word that you can declare (pray out loud) to counteract the lie?

A Prayer in the Processing

Lord, I bring every one of these thoughts to you and submit them to you. Fill my mind with whatever is pure and lovely, whatever produces good fruit in my and my family's lives. I reject every word of the enemy and declare that I am holding on to your truth. You told me to cast my burdens on you because you care about me—and I am determined to do that again and again. I give it all to you.

Thank you for hearing me, thank you for helping me, thank you for filling me. In Jesus's name, amen.

Chapter 6

Examining Our Spiritual Foundations

Therefore everyone who hears these words of mine and puts them into practice is like a wise man who built his house on the rock. The rain came down, the streams rose, and the winds blew and beat against that house; yet it did not fall, because it had its foundation on the rock. But everyone who hears these words of mine and does not put them into practice is like a foolish man who built his house on sand. The rain came down, the streams rose, and the winds blew and beat against that house, and it fell with a great crash.

—Matthew 7:24–27

Long before Graham passed, Jesse and I had made a decision that no matter how our lives went, our goal was to build them on God's truth and hold fast to his Word. This was going to be our foundation and a preset in our lives. That didn't mean we always had perfect execution, but it was our heart's desire!

In the life of a believer, loss tends to make us examine the foundation of our faith. In good times we may say God is good, the devil has no place in our lives, and we are the righteousness of God in Christ Jesus, but what happens when a storm shakes up our world? Are we able to hold fast to these truths with the same tenacity? As this parable outlines, how we have built leading up to this point is important. The benefits of putting God's Word into practice and building our spiritual homes on the rock are clear.

Equally important, however, is how we interpret the storm itself. As believers, we can, indeed, expect great blessings and benefits in our lives. And in the end, we will stand firm because of a solid foundation. However, a hardship-free life is not promised. Ultimately Jesus said the storm would come, that we "will have trouble" (John 16:33). We cannot interpret storms in our lives to mean that we aren't built on the rock or that there is something wrong with the house. Imagine how ridiculous it would be for someone to blame a house for a storm!

Some of you reading this will think that, because you have questions you can't find answers to, because you have overwhelming feelings, because your insides feel chaotic, that you are going through a crisis of faith. You may feel that you didn't build as well as you thought you did. I would like to remind you that even the most sturdily built home has aftermath to deal with.

In post-loss life you may be examining parts of your faith you never did before because there was never a problem. But now there are shingles missing, debris inside the home, siding that needs to be replaced—you get the picture! Don't mistake a house in need of repair with a house that is condemned. One needs clean-up and the skill of the good Carpenter. The other is uninhabitable. The fact that you are reading this book tells me that you are seeing the debris and recognizing something needs to be done. You are recognizing your starting point. That is a good thing!

Unfortunately most of us have probably witnessed tragic outcomes for believers after trauma or loss. Those who seemingly abandon their faith or change what they think about God after they go through tragedy. We could say that it's a foundation issue, but I actually think most of the time it comes down to how we handle the questions in the aftermath of the storm. When I think back to Graham's passing, Jesse and I were in a healthy church environment. Yet even in a good environment, we had to work through some pivotal questions with the Lord. I will discuss those in detail, but before I do, let's talk about a few stumbling blocks that can prevent you from even getting to the questions in the first place.

Faith Facade

Some believers find it uncomfortable to engage with questions of faith that arise after a loss. For them it may be easier to put up a faith facade, quoting Scripture or a cliche Christian phrase when someone asks them how they are doing. Instead of addressing their own uncomfortable theological questions, they see these questions as weaknesses or threats to their faith. The result is that the house is not repaired or cleaned up, only covered up, making the home susceptible to internal weakness. Quoting Scripture is good! Using Scripture as a defense mechanism to not process grief with the Lord is not. In many cases I have seen a faith facade repel comfort, not only from people, but also from God, because it says in essence, "I don't need your work here, I'm fine."

Deconstruction or Destruction Mode

I have seen other believers go into destruction mode, often after putting up a faith facade for quite some time. The problem is they look good from the outside, while the inside of the house is still unrepaired. Other people

CREATIVE COMFORT

may see a cleaned-up house, but internally the person knows something is not right. *But I'm doing what a good Christian is supposed to do,* they may think. As internal damage continues to fester, extreme disappointment, bitterness, and anger sets in. *Well, if this is how it's going to be, then forget it!* Even if their house is still standing, I have seen people begin to assist the destroyer and tear their own house down. Not only did their relationship with God dissolve, but also their relationship with their spouse, other family, or close friends.

"Condemned House" Theology

I have seen still others who have downgraded their view of God and their belief about his nature because they couldn't reconcile what they believed about God with how things turned out for them personally. Where they once believed in the goodness of God, perhaps now they believe that God isn't much involved in our personal lives or that he allows or even causes evil. They think: *If he didn't, how could this have happened?* In this example, the house never gets cleaned up; they just live in the mess, believing it is the best they can expect in life.

I think most of us can identify our own tendencies toward unhealthy processing, but the point is not to feel bad about it. The point is to be aware and understand that this does not have to be your experience if you don't want it to be! Even if you have started out on the wrong foot, God can turn it around if we would just ask him. As a child of God, he wants your journey to be so much richer, so much more life-giving. We just have to know that it is available to us and approach the Lord in faith. Grief is personal, and God wants to get personal with you in your uncomfortable questions and feelings. I encourage you to lean into it.

Lean into him. Approach him boldly, even if you don't exactly know what to say.

Before we get to those questions, there is a root truth that must be reaffirmed in our hearts: the Bible is the ultimate source of truth. From the Old Testament to the New Testament, do we believe it to be everything we need for "life and godliness," as it says in 2 Peter 1:3? I think it's interesting that the first temptation of man by Satan was in the Garden of Eden when he approached Eve: "Did God really say . . .?" The first thing that he attacked was the validity of God's Word to them. In the face of our worldly difficulties and trials, do we really think the enemy's tactics have changed? I would say that they have not.

Believing the Bible as the ultimate source of truth is the foundation of Christianity and of our faith in God. Some question the validity of parts of the Bible, yet say they believe in the complete salvation work of Jesus. If Jesus was called the "Word made flesh," I don't know that I would feel comfortable leaving parts of that Word out! To believe the Bible is the ultimate truth is to believe that Jesus is the ultimate salvation. There can be things we don't understand, and that's okay. There can be perceived contradictions that make us ask questions, and that's okay. But don't be so quick to label it, and most importantly don't stay there and fester. Questions come up for a reason—so that we can be seekers of truth. Don't fall for the trap of seeking conclusions at the cost of truth. This may satisfy our desire for certainty but undermine our walk with the Lord. We weren't meant to have all the answers. Instead, we should be seekers of the Lord, of truth at any cost. Spoiler alert: he is the truth!

If the enemy can't make you question the validity of the Word of God, he will try to make you a victim of skewed theology. I find it interesting that when the enemy tempted Jesus in the wilderness, he used

God's Word to do it. "'If you are the Son of God,' he said, 'throw your-self down. For it is written: "He will command his angels concerning you, and they will lift you up in their hands, so that you will not strike your foot against a stone"'" (Matt. 4:6). He knew that Jesus would not question the validity of God's Word, or he would not have used it to tempt Jesus. Instead, he presented skewed and out-of-context truth in the hopes that he could bait Jesus into doing something foolish. Jesus not only knew the craftiness of his enemy, he also knew the character of his Father. He turned it on the enemy in the next verse, "It is also writ-ten: 'Do not put the Lord your God to the test'" (Matt. 4:7).

I challenge you not to get your theology from popular mainstream teachings or social media sound bites, which can contain incomplete truths and contextually inaccurate premises. In the back of this book, I will be adding information on additional resources from biblical schol-ars that have helped me build a strong foundation in my Christian walk. I encourage you to check them out. In my personal wilderness, the Word of God has not only been my foundation but a powerful weapon in my hand. Don't be robbed of this weapon because of lack of understanding, misconceptions, or popular half-truths. Maybe there is something you heard years ago that is still negatively affecting your faith today. If there is anything to question—question that! Even if some of what the Bible says goes beyond our current understanding, we can still activate and apply our faith in advance, knowing that God will give us revelation as we seek him and "study to show ourselves approved" (2 Tim. 2:15).

When it comes to faith, God makes it clear that faith does not need to see something to believe. It does not even need to experience some-thing to believe. In the Old Testament, God made a promise to Abra-ham that he would be a father of many nations. The Bible says that

"Abraham believed God, and it was credited to him as righteousness" (Rom. 4:3). Did you know that this so-called "father of many nations" only had one son himself and two grandchildren? He did not see anything close to fulfillment of the full promise, but he still believed, having confidence in God's nature and character. All of Hebrews 11 talks about those who were commended for their faith without receiving what was promised. As humans we tend to think in scales of our lifetime, but God's timetable is much different. Even so, he is a God of his Word.

Post-resurrection Jesus said to his disciple Thomas, "blessed are those who have not seen and yet have believed" (John 20:29). This is, in fact, the foundation of our Christian faith. We who have not seen Jesus for ourselves, believe! There is great blessing in that space. We have to realize that the faith we apply to believing in the salvation work of Jesus is the same faith we have the opportunity to apply to principles in his Word that we may not yet understand. We can still trust God and put faith in his nature without knowing every answer.

Questions to ponder:

1. What parts of your faith foundation are you re-examining post-loss?

2. Can you identify any unhealthy tendencies in your grief processing (faith facade, destruction/deconstruction mode, "condemned house" theology or something else)?

3. What are some ways can you apply your faith even when you lack understanding or answers?

A prayer in the processing

Lord, thank you for helping me examine my own spiritual foundation. Help me see through appearances and view the clean-up with your eyes. I will be honest Lord, sometimes it feels overwhelming. But I know you are the good Carpenter and you aren't going to leave me here. I open my heart to your work. Help me to seek you as the truth when I don't have many answers, and sometimes don't know what to say. Just like our spiritual forefathers didn't see yet believed, so will I! I am determined to seek you as the truth and allow you to bring clarity in your timing. I trust you Lord. In Jesus's name, amen.

Chapter 7

Asking the Real Questions

Jesus doesn't give an explanation for the pain and sorrow of the world. He comes where the pain is most acute and takes it upon himself. Jesus doesn't explain why there is suffering, illness, and death in the world. He brings healing and hope. He doesn't allow the problem of evil to be the subject of a seminar. He allows evil to do its worst to him. He exhausts it, drains its power, and emerges with new life.[3]

N. T. Wright, *Simply Good News: Why the Gospel is News and What Makes it Good*

It's important to know that faith questions will naturally arise as part of your grieving process. As we talked about in the last chapter, handling them in spiritually healthy ways is one of the most important things we can do. But what does that mean, exactly? For one, it means we must dig past "I know what's true in my head, so that should be good enough for me." Isn't that a "good" Christian response before we shove down our emotions?

In my own faith walk there have been times when I have known truth but lamented that my emotions wouldn't automatically fall in line. It's for that reason that we can't just ignore our questions or emotions;

we must work through them with the Word of God as our foundation and the Holy Spirit as our helper. Part of the working out of our salvation, which is a continual process, involves being patient with the whole head-to-heart journey. The Holy Spirit opens our hearts to accept truth in faith, but our understanding comes as we "work it out" in our lives. Like the main character in the Parable of the Sower, we often need the ground of our hearts plowed up in order for the truth to take root.

If you find yourself bumping into questions that you don't have answers for, please know this is normal. Life events like loss tend to make us question a lot of things. It's not something to feel bad about; it's something that should prompt us to seek the Lord. God is not afraid of our questions. In fact, he wants us to ask! Pray for help, seek out wisdom from God's Word and seasoned believers who are full of the Holy Spirit.

For Jesse and me, it was pivotal to be surrounded by likeminded believers in a church that not only taught sound doctrine and theology but also operated in the gifts and power of the Holy Spirit. It was an environment of health that provided the context for healthy grief processing. Even more than that, we found a place where our whole lives were ministered to as our faith continued to be sharpened. We needed grief care, but we also needed whole life care and to continue to be challenged in our faith. The context for grief is so very important. We must be connected to the life-giving source of God's Spirit within a body of believers.

Grief can be complicated, with lots of complicated emotions and seemingly complicated questions. Healthy processing involves taking those complicated questions and examining the root. A person who feels anger (and may even say they are angry at God) may ask, *"How could God have let this happen?"* But is that actually the question? The root question is probably closer to, *"Is God who I thought he was? Is he actually good?"* And the anger? That may be a layer in our emotions, but the root is probably closer to pain mixed with severe disappointment. I will be talking about some of my root questions in a moment, but for me personally, pain and severe disappointment (along with embarrassment, strangely) were root emotions for me when I was walking through grief. However, knowing that freed me and allowed me to come to the Father as I actually was, not as I perceived myself to be.

If you think about your own questions and they feel overwhelming to you, it is likely a sign that there is room to simplify. Invite the Holy Spirit into your processing and ask him to help you get to the root. Expect there to be emotions because it's an emotional process! Just know it's not about being hyper-fixated on finding answers. It's about seeking the Lord as the answer and allowing him to bring clarity to your heart and mind in his timing. As I sought the Lord in my own processing, I found that my questions boiled down to a few themes, which I wanted to share with you in the next chapter. The first thing you might notice is that they are pretty basic. This is on purpose. In my own grief processing I asked the Lord to show me how to address the root questions or truths. The wonderful thing is, as I sought him about this, he showed these roots to me, and I found a strengthening of my foundations that I had never known before.

Before I dive into them though, I wanted to take you through a little exercise to write down your questions. First, write down your "knee-jerk" questions—the ones that are closest to the surface, maybe even the most emotionally charged. At the end, we'll revisit and make sure we have the root ones!

1.

2.

3.

4.

5.

A prayer in the processing:

Lord, thank you that you meant for me to run to you with my biggest questions. As I write them down here, would you show me the roots? I want to process each one with you and I know you want to minister to my heart. Thank you for helping me as I seek you as the truth and the answer. In Jesus's name, amen.

Chapter 8

My Root Questions

Oh, taste and see that the Lord is good; blessed is the man who trusts in Him!

—Psalm 34:8 NKJV

Is God Good?

Many of you probably know this scripture and others like it. God's representation of himself in his Word is that he is good! I have thought a lot about this over the years, especially in the context of post-loss life. The tensions between knowing the goodness of God, while also dealing with your own personal tragedy, is nothing to downplay. In my questions, this was the first truth that needed to be reaffirmed. One of our greatest temptations in loss is to change how we think about the character and nature of God to fit our circumstances. Often it is human nature to revert to the easiest and most quickly arrived-at answer. However, it is far better to come to terms with the fact that there are some things that we may not understand immediately or ever, but the opportunity to apply our faith using God's Word as our foundation remains.

Ultimately, God is God. We are human. Can we ever be expected to comprehend the magnitude of his nature and ways? Can mortal minds really comprehend the infinitude of the One who created them? The book of Revelation tells us that even angelic beings in heaven are constantly singing "holy, holy, holy!" Some theologians have written that every time they circle the throne, they see a new side of his character. In doing so they can't help but be overwhelmed by his muchness, his endlessness, his eternalness. As big as the universe is, even the magnitude we know it to be cannot come close to the endlessness of our God. Scientists say that since the beginning, our universe has never stopped expanding. Think about that. It continues to grow beyond our solar system, beyond our galaxy, beyond a million galaxies. Is there a God who carries more substance than that? It's truly overwhelming to think about.

We live in a world that likes to make everything "figure-out-able" and tends to oversimplify complex matters. We do this with the Creator of heaven and earth too! *Did something turn out well for me?* Then God is good. *Did something not turn out well for me?* It must mean God is not as good as I thought. When something like tragic loss happens, these questions tend to move to the forefront. However, the questions that come up after a tragic loss or event are the same that have been asked by humans in different forms over the millennia. It's what happens when we read the truth of God's Word but then look around us and see a world full of things that seem to contradict what we read about his character in the Bible and perhaps our own ideals of how things should be. *"If God's so good, then why is there war and disaster on the earth?"* Or, *"If God really heals people, then why aren't the hospitals cleared out?"* Or, *"If God blesses those who follow him, why did this bad thing happen to me?"*

There are two things at play here. The first is an understanding of the nature of the kingdom of God. We all know that in the beginning God created the earth and put two humans in a perfect paradise called the Garden of Eden. Adam and Eve walked in perfect communion with

God until they fell prey to the trickery of the serpent and ate fruit from the tree of the knowledge of good and evil. Through their disobedience, sin was introduced onto the earth, along with everything sin brings— chaos, death, destruction. Accounts from the Bible show that life for mankind from that point on was extremely difficult. The world was far from the perfection that had first initiated it. Fast forward through the Old Testament and into the New, and we see Jesus the Son of God coming onto the scene. His ministry had been heralded by John the Baptist, who told people to repent because "the kingdom of God has come near" (Mark 1:15).

Something was breaking onto the scene that humans had never seen before—the inauguration of the kingdom of God! The plan that God had from the very beginning was going to be enacted through the God-man Jesus Christ.

We know the rest of the story. Jesus came to give us life and life more abundantly. His death and resurrection, then subsequent sending of the Holy Spirit, was the initiation of a new age on earth—the age of the in-breaking kingdom of God. An inherent characteristic of this kingdom was an idea theologians know of as "now and not yet." The kingdom of God had been initiated, so it was "now" but the fullness of it was "not yet." Even Jesus said in Matthew 13:31–32, "The kingdom of heaven is like a mustard seed, which a man took and planted in his field. Though it is the smallest of all seeds, yet when it grows, it is the largest of garden plants and becomes a tree, so that the birds come and perch in its branches." It was about growing, about advancing, through the children of the kingdom!

The second thing to understand is that although the kingdom has been increasing and growing ever since its initiation, our world is still not perfect. Imperfect things still happen. I remember sitting in a theology class when one of my teachers was speaking about the kingdom of God. He stood in front of the room, making reference to the "tensions of the kingdom," his hands seeming to pull on opposite sides of an invisible string. That is the best explanation for our life on earth. Humans are not exactly comfortable with tensions. Oftentimes we take the most obvious story and run with it. It happened with the Jews in Jesus's day. Did you know that the Jews were not opposed to having a messiah? They wanted one! In fact, there had been many "messiahs" prior to Jesus who promised victory over their mortal enemies and oppressors, the Romans. These "messiahs" had led revolts and rebellions in attempts to free the Jews, but none to any success. So when Jesus came along, they thought just maybe this was the man who was going to call down the fire of heaven to consume their enemies, not realizing he was there to address a different enemy. Jesus was both a lion and a lamb. A lion to those religious leaders who loaded down the people of God with rules too heavy to bear. A lamb to those oppressed and lost in a religious system that had ceased to minister to or care for them. They wanted to deal with an enemy without, but there was an enemy within that needed to be addressed.

We similarly have tensions in our own day. The tension of seeing miraculous healings take place (and I have!), but also not seeing everyone healed. The tension of seeing other children saved out of the jaws of death (and I have!), and not understanding what happened with my own son. Ultimately, we believe and pray for the absolute best, applying our faith to what we know is true from the Word of God. We believe that, just like Deuteronomy 28 says, those who serve the Lord will be blessed beyond measure. That doesn't always mean perfect circumstances, but it means that no matter what we go through, the character of God does not change and he is always there to help us.

We won't see 100 percent of the fullness of the kingdom or a con-summation of these tensions until Jesus returns. God's will is for break-through, healing, and rescue to happen. But imperfection still exists. Does this mean we give up? No! Does it mean we are insecure about God's intention? Not a chance. It means we continue to apply our faith, believing for and declaring God's absolute best, knowing that God has given us every tool we need for the worst. Even when we don't fully un-derstand the "why," we can call on his name and be equipped to face any giant in our way.

Was It the Enemy?

After reaffirming the truth of God's goodness, the next question made its way into my mind: "Then, what happened?" If God is good and only does good, was the enemy somehow involved? As we revisit a few verses we have already talked about, the Bible makes it clear what the enemy's goal is:

The thief comes only to steal and kill and destroy... (John 10:10)

Be alert and of sober mind. Your enemy the devil prowls around like a roaring lion looking for someone to devour. (1 Pet. 5:8)

Based on the outcome alone, of course Jesse and I did feel robbed. Robbed of years with our son, robbed of joy, robbed of fruitfulness. However, our spirits revolted at the thought that the enemy had "gotten" Graham. It didn't make sense, but what happened if not?

In the late summer following Graham's passing, Jesse and I were at a local restaurant talking about this. It had been a rough week, and it was a beautiful day, so we decided to eat outside. On that particular day, this question had come to the forefront again. As we talked the tears flowed. I told Jesse how I knew God didn't take Graham from us, but I also didn't feel like the enemy had "gotten" him either. The words were coming out of my mouth, when out of the corner of my eye I saw a woman we knew from church walking toward us. But this wasn't just anyone. We saw this same woman almost every time we went somewhere. We would be at the grocery store in another town, and we would see her there. We would walk into Target, and we would see her there. We would grab coffee at a coffee shop, and she just so happened to be there at the same time. Every time we saw her she would always have a word of encouragement, a word of knowledge, a prayer, or something prophetic to say. It was absolutely uncanny, but it was a creative way God ministered to us.

When we saw her this time, Jesse and I both started to laugh. Of course we would see her here too! We hugged, chit-chatted, and laughed about how we were constantly bumping into one another and how we knew it was the Lord. Inevitably the conversation turned to Graham when out of the blue and completely unprompted she said, "The enemy doesn't get any credit for this. Graham belonged to the Lord." We were dumbfounded. She continued, "I give the enemy about two seconds before I kick him to the curb!" Talk about a word for where we were right then. She didn't know that we had just been talking about that. The fact that this person had spoken directly to our conversation without knowing it was a confirmation. Sometimes we don't know everything that is, but in that moment God confirmed what was not.

Most of us know the story of Job. Some could point to that story alone as proof that the enemy can mess with the life of a believer and even steal and rob from us at will. However, we must remember who had authority in the earth when Job was alive. The enemy ruled because man gave up his authority when he sinned in the Garden. It wasn't until Jesus came that the "kingdom of the world has become the kingdom of our Lord and of his Messiah" (Rev. 11:15). With Jesus's death and resurrection, he took the keys to death, hell, and the grave. He restored the authority lost in the Garden. The enemy still acts as an outlaw and renegade on earth, but without the real authority God has placed in the lives of the believers.

The moment of talking to our friend was all we needed to confirm God's Word in our hearts. It was such a sweet surprise, a creative ministry from the Lord, that we will always treasure. We had already had a sense of the truth, but God saw us, he knew, and he wanted to bring clarity.

There are some things you may feel that you know intuitively by the Holy Spirit, but perhaps it doesn't feel confirmed or settled. That's okay. As we seek the Lord, we open the door for him to creatively minister to us and bring clarity in his timing. The wonderful thing is also the not-wonderful thing: we don't know exactly how or when he will do it! But as we trust him with our journey and our questions, we open ourselves to his creative work in our lives. Be sure it will always take us by surprise!

Was it Us?

A question that came up almost simultaneously with "Was it the enemy?" was about our responsibility as parents. Had we somehow opened a spiritual door that allowed this to happen?

Depending on your background, this may not be a question for you. I have heard messages that seemed to imply that what do here on earth doesn't matter. As long as we believe Jesus Christ is Lord, we will be saved and anything more than that is just us trying to earn our salvation. Although this thought contains the foundational truth of Jesus Christ as our salvation, it seems to ignore all of the New Testament after the gospels, which shows us how to live after coming to know Christ. Of course, we can't earn salvation! But as children of God and representatives of a new kingdom on earth, what we do has spiritual weight and should not to be taken lightly.

In Ephesians 4, Paul outlines instructions for Christian living:

> So I tell you this, and insist on it in the Lord, that you must no longer live as the Gentiles do, in the futility of their thinking. They are darkened in their understanding and separated from the life of God because of the ignorance that is in them due to the hardening of their hearts. Having lost all sensitivity, they have given themselves over to sensuality so as to indulge in every kind of impurity, and they are full of greed.
>
> That, however, is not the way of life you learned when you heard about Christ and were taught in him in accordance with the truth that is in Jesus. You were taught, with regard to your former way of life, to put off your old self, which is being corrupted by its deceitful desires; to be made new in the attitude of your minds; and to put on the new self, created to be like God in true righteousness and holiness. (v. 17–24)

I find it interesting that Paul refers to "the way of life you learned when you heard about Christ" (vss. 20–21). That means he is revisiting some past truths and reminding them: "don't go back to your old self, be made new!" The verses following outline how we should live with and speak to one another. If God didn't care how we lived, why would he would go to all that trouble to convert Paul then use him to write half of the New Testament, which was written to believers by the way? Of course, we are made new when we receive Christ, but we must purpose to keep walking in that path and make decisions that don't fight against the nature of God inside of us or our children or open up spiritual doors to chaos.

Looking back at our precious time with Graham, I remember praying for him every day—for protection, that he would grow up to be strong in the Lord, that he would know his godly identity. We had received so many encouraging personal words about him and from others. I still have a note in my phone with the dates and specifics of those words. We had blessed him constantly. You could say we had done everything "right." And even despite that, the worst had happened. There were more than a few times when I thought, *Certainly we were entitled to some protection?* But in a split second afterward I would remember Jesus's words, "in this world you will have trouble" (John 16:33). He was referring to persecution, and most of the people he was speaking to were eventually martyred for Christ. If the Lord, himself, and the disciples had trouble, then how could we expect no hardships?

I find it amazing that we read a story in the Bible, take it at face value, and accept its simple truths, but we often struggle to do the same with our own story, especially when we're in the middle of it. I am going to be talking about the account of Job in more detail in a moment, but before I go there, think about this: Did the fact that Job went through so many horrors reveal a lack of righteousness on his part? Did his present circumstances mean that God was any less good, or that the blessings of his former life were not really God-given? No.

How about a New Testament example? Luke 13 starts off with Jesus being told of some Galileans who had been killed and their blood was mixed with Pontius Pilate's sacrifices. Jesus answered: "Do you think that these Galileans were worse sinners than all the other Galileans because they suffered this way? I tell you, no! . . . Or those eighteen who died when the tower of Siloam fell on them—do you think they were more guilty than all the others living in Jerusalem? I tell you, no!" (vss. 2–5).

Jesus appeared to be completely unconcerned that the present circumstances seemed to contradict what his audience thought they knew about God. When it comes to our own story, it causes us to examine the simple truths we formerly accepted. If this has happened to me, is God actually good? Or, if you are convinced of his goodness, maybe you've begun to wonder if you've done something to deserve this? The truth is if God killed everyone on earth for sinning, then there would be no one left. We have all sinned and fallen short of the glory of God. As people who love the Lord and are doing our best to serve him, our conclusion can only be the same as these biblical examples. In short, bad things happen and it's not always explainable. But even in the midst of the tragedy, who do we say God is?

After loss, the story of Job took on new meaning for me. Job was a righteous man who went through unspeakable hardship, trials beyond understanding. He lost all of his children, his health, his wealth, and his friends. The only friends who remained constantly questioned him and his motives in his darkest hour. There are some 42 chapters dedicated to his experience, and it's painful to read. But Job is a reminder of how very real the battle is for our hearts and devotion. The enemy does everything he can to besmirch and mar the image of God on the earth, and if he can cause us to turn on God or lower our level of devotion because of tragedy or disappointment, it is a high prize for him, indeed.

When the enemy came before the Lord in Job 1, God said:

> "Have you considered my servant Job? There is no one on earth like him; he is blameless and upright, a man who fears God and shuns evil."
>
> "Does Job fear God for nothing? Satan replied. "Have you not put a hedge around him and his household and everything he has? You have blessed the work of his hands, so that his flocks and herds are spread throughout the land. But now stretch out your hand and strike everything he has, and he will surely curse you to your face." (Job 1:8–11)

The chapters that follow take us through Job's story of great loss. Within twenty-four hours, he lost all of his children and his property. However, in Job 1:22, it says, "In all of this, Job did not sin by charging God with wrongdoing."

Then the accuser came before the Lord again:

> Then the LORD said to Satan, "Have you considered my servant Job? There is no one on earth like him; he is blameless and upright, a man who fears God and shuns evil. And he still maintains his integrity, though you incited me against him to ruin him without any reason."

CREATIVE COMFORT

"Skin for skin!" Satan replied. "A man will give all he has for his own life. But now stretch out your hand and strike his flesh and bones, and he will surely curse you to your face." (Job 2:3–5)

At that point, Job was struck with terrible boils from head to foot. Talk about insult to injury!

Many of you know the rest of the story . . . his wife tells him to just curse God and die. His friends spend tens of chapters questioning Job's motives and not giving good representations of God's character. However, Job maintains his innocence through it all. He even says:

As long as I have life within me,
    the breath of God in my nostrils,
my lips will not say anything wicked,
    and my tongue will not utter lies.
I will never admit you [the friends] are in the right;
    til I die, I will not deny my integrity.
I will maintain my innocence and never let go of it;
    my conscience will not reproach me as long as I live.
(Job 27:3–6)

The story ends with God being angry with Job's friends because they did not speak accurately about God "as my servant Job has." At the conclusion of the story, God has Job pray for his friends! When Job does this, "the Lord restored his fortunes and gave him twice as much as he had before." Innumerable flocks and herds, and seven more sons and three daughters. Talk about restoration!

When I read that story before going through loss myself, it sounded like a huge win for Job, and it was. Job maintained his innocence, he refused to blame the Lord, and in the end God restored it all . . . and then some. However, when I read the story after Graham passed away, it occurred to me that Job's children didn't come back from the dead. What was lost was still lost on this side of heaven. However, I think God did something in Job's heart so that he could receive restoration, which I think is especially relevant for those walking through grief today. So often grief tells us that we will never really live again, that our experience on earth will always be tainted by the devastation of loss. But when I meditate on the story of Job, it encourages me. I have a job to do here: to see my story through God's lens, to bring my whole heart to the Lord no matter what, and to cast every burden, every question, every tear on him. That's something God can work with.

Sometimes there is more going on than meets the eye, and that is absolutely the case for believers who have experienced loss and are taking their grief to the Lord. It will take time, as it did for Job, but as we position our hearts before him, God has promised to help us and restore our souls.

Questions to Ponder

Look back at the questions you wrote in chapter 7. Have they changed to get closer to the root? If so, write them here:

1.

2.

3.

4.

5.

A Prayer in the Processing

Lord, I bring each of these questions to you. Thank you for helping me get to the root of what I am thinking and feeling so you can minister to me where I really am. I admit that I don't have all the answers, but as I seek you as the Truth and the Answer, I believe you are bringing clarity and understanding to my heart. Help me to be patient with that process. I look to you and wait on you, Lord. I love you. In Jesus's name, amen.

Chapter 9

Turmoil That Produces

⁓◌

Let's be honest, no one likes turmoil. Unfortunately, the experience of walking through grief is rife with it. There's no escaping it. The question then is: what do we do with it?

We have the opportunity to express our grief in ways that are like an offering before the Lord. For me, no matter what the particular expression of grief looked like, I always made it clear to the Lord that I was pouring it out to him. If my heart was going to break in pieces, it was going to break before him. This was more than just a release of emotion; it was an offering. I wanted him to know that it was an offering but that I also expected something in return. The Bible says the Lord is a friend who sticks closer than a brother, that he is a comforter (Prov. 18:24). If that was the case, I was expecting him to be that for me!

Grief is awkward all around, but sometimes it was especially uncomfortable and awkward to be so raw before the Lord. If there was one thing I did "right" in this whole process, however, it's that I never sought to get myself out of it or hurry it up. I decided early on that I was going to sit in the awkwardness until the Lord helped me. David said in Psalm 51:17, "My sacrifice, O God, is a broken spirit; a broken and contrite heart you, God, will not despise." If I was going to be broken, then I decided it was going to be my sacrifice. I offered my broken heart to him so many times.

There is really no other time in my life that I felt undone in my personality and in my heart, but at the same time I felt the nearness and the delight of the Lord. My heart would be in a puddle on the floor before him, yet I would feel the real, tangible presence of God pulling me close and bringing deep comfort to my soul.

It turns out there is some biblical precedent for this, although it requires us to read perhaps familiar Scriptures with new eyes. First Samuel gives an account of a woman named Hannah who was married to a man named Elkanah. Hannah was childless, but Elkanah's other wife, Peninnah, bore him several children. It says that Peninnah would continually provoke Hannah about this fact in order to irritate her. This seemed to be heightened each year when the family would travel to Shiloh to make their annual sacrifice. "Whenever Hannah went up to the house of the LORD, her rival provoked her till she wept and would not eat" (1 Sam. 1:7). The Bible said it went on year after year, but especially when Hannah went up to the house of the Lord. It said that her rival would provoke her until she wept. How awful! The story continues:

> Once when they had finished eating and drinking in Shiloh, Hannah stood up. Now Eli the priest was sitting on his chair by the doorpost of the LORD's house. In her deep anguish Hannah prayed to the LORD, weeping bitterly. And she made a vow, saying, "LORD Almighty, if you will only look on your servant's misery and remember me, and not forget your servant but give her a son, then I will give him to the LORD for all the days of his life, and no razor will ever be used on his head."
>
> As she kept on praying to the LORD, Eli observed her mouth. Hannah was praying in her heart, and her lips were moving but

her voice was not heard. Eli thought she was drunk and said to her, "How long are you going to stay drunk? Put away your wine."

"Not so, my lord," Hannah replied, "I am a woman who is deeply troubled. I have not been drinking wine or beer; I was pouring out my soul to the LORD. Do not take your servant for a wicked woman; I have been praying here out of my great anguish and grief." (1 Sam 1:9–16)

I don't know about you, but the verbiage around her prayer sounds an awful lot like an offering of grief to me. So often in the story of Hannah we focus on the ultimate promise fulfilled but not the process it took to get there. Hannah was not afraid to lay her soul bare before the Lord. "In her deep anguish Hannah prayed to the Lord, weeping bitterly," it says. When Eli, the priest, saw her praying, he thought she was drunk, but Hannah was so provoked that it prompted her to pour out what the Bible calls a "complaint" before the Lord.

Eli answered, "Go in peace, and may the God of Israel grant you what you have asked of him" (v. 17). I think it's interesting here that Eli didn't say, "You know the promises God gave to the Israelites through Moses. Keep declaring them until you feel better." Hannah was obviously a covenant person. She knew Scripture; she knew the promises. But she was a covenant person in turmoil.

I believe what we do with that turmoil is a deciding factor in how our grief journey plays out. When we don't take real grief and anguish to the Lord, our only options are to: grit our teeth and try to get through in our own strength; to stew in our anguish and sorrow as we try and fail not to be triggered by circumstances and then feel bad for feeling bad; to pacify, distract, or numb ourselves away from reality; or to resign ourselves to the fact that we will always be broken people because of what we went through.

Like I mentioned earlier, I have seen those who try to put on a "faith facade."

The kind who will always quote Scripture when someone asks them a question about how they're doing. There will always be some upside to what they're going through: "God is just wanting me to minister to other people, that's why I'm experiencing this tragedy." Don't get me wrong, God can use anything for his glory, and even in tragedy he can turn it around for good. That is one of the miraculous things about serving the Lord. However, we really need to reexamine our theology if we believe that everything we go through it to teach us or other people a lesson. Can you imagine an earthly father doing that? No way! And God says he is much better than that.

In our own processing we need to make sure we are grounded in good biblical precedent. The Bible never said to cast your cares upon the Lord "in theory" or to keep a stiff upper lip so people know how strong and full of faith you are. It was a command to give our tears to God in reality and receive something in return. If it was only meant to be something nice to say and not something you actually feel, wouldn't God tell us that?

The amazing thing is that even before Hannah received the fulfillment of the promise, she received something from the Lord. 1 Samuel 1:18 says, "She went her way and ate something, and her face was no longer downcast." What had materially changed since before Hannah had prayed? Technically nothing. Even Eli was clueless, and he basically just said, "Well, I hope you get your prayer answered." However, in that moment Hannah received something tangible from the Lord that changed the way she felt and even looked! That is the goal in our outpouring to the Lord. We give it all to him, but we receive something in return that changes our outlook just like Hannah did.

The issue sometimes is our own mental blockage and poor theology about how to "do grief right." From what I can read in Scripture, though, God is pleased with those who pour out their hearts and anguish, or "complain," to him. We were never meant to keep going around the mountain of misery endlessly; we were meant to pour it out before the Lord.

I love how raw David and the other Psalmists get:

I cry aloud to the Lord;
I lift up my voice to the Lord for mercy.
I pour out before him my complaint;
before him I tell my trouble. (Psalm 142:1–2)

But I cry to you for help, Lord;
in the morning my prayer comes before you.
Why, Lord, do You reject me
and hide your face from me?
From my youth I have suffered and been close to death;
I have borne your terrors and am in despair;
Your wrath has swept over me; your terrors have destroyed me.
All day long they surround me like a flood; they have completely engulfed me.
You have taken from me friend and neighbor -
darkness is my closest friend. (Ps. 88:13–18, emphasis mine)

Sheesh, that seems a little dark, right? Yet it ended up in the Bible as an example for us!

Do we preclude ourselves from this kind of outpouring because we think of it more as poetry, instead of being the real and raw outpouring it was? Were not Hannah, David, and the Psalmists humans like us? Is God not the same God? Is there not something causing anguish in our souls?

We need to be people who aren't afraid to knock at our Father's door with our grief. We are a people in covenant with him; our foundation is his Word, and he commands us to come boldly. Even if you have to come shaking in your boots because you're not sure what is allowed—tell him that! Tell him you're not quite sure how to approach him. He appreciates that honesty and your desire for connection more than he does your presuming that you can't bring certain thoughts and emotions to him. The amazing thing is that, as you seek him out, as you ask him, you are going to find him bringing you a clarity and a deeper knowledge of him. Sometimes we just need the Holy Spirit to breathe on what we already know (in our heads) about his character and make it a reality in our hearts:

> Ask and it will be given to you; seek and you will find; knock and the door will be opened to you. For everyone who asks receives; the one who seeks finds; and to the one who knocks, the door will be opened. Which of you, if your son asks for bread, will give him a stone? Or if he asks for a fish, will give him a snake? If you, then, though you are evil, know how to give good gifts to your children, how much more will your Father in heaven give good gifts to those who ask him! (Matt. 7:7–11)

How many of you know there is a difference in the types of knocking . . . there is a difference in the urgency of a polite little rap on the door and urgent, assaulting-the-door type knocking. It says to those who knock, the door will be opened. Just being honest, I am not going to open the door for a polite little knock from a solicitor or UPS. But if someone I love is urgently pounding on my door, nothing is going to make me get up off the couch and run faster.

When notable people in the Bible had something they needed from the Lord, they always approached him on the basis of their covenant relationship and decided that they would and could not be satisfied with anything else, and that they would lay it all out before the Lord. God isn't looking for us to come with matter-of-fact requests in which we state our case and mechanically back it up with Scripture. He wants us to come to him and pour out our desire, pour out our heartbreak, pour out our restraint before him. We need to be people who aren't afraid to knock at our Father's door with very real needs, frustrations, and grievances. We are people in covenant with him, we stand on his Word, and he commands us to come boldly.

The truth is this: God is a good Father. He wants us to come to Him about everything but especially the hard stuff, the grievous stuff. Imagine being a parent and saying, "I only want you to praise me for the good stuff happening in your life, but if there is something challenging or hard, I want you to tell me the Scripture you're standing on and put on a happy face in faith." The patriarchs and matriarchs in the faith never had this mindset. They were never afraid to fully feel their circumstances, probably in ways that, to our Western minds, border on unbelief.

David says in Psalm 5: "Listen to my words, LORD, consider my lament. Hear my cry for help, my King and my God, for to you I pray"

(v. 1–2). This isn't even one of his more blunt psalms, but it's a good one to take your own temperature. Have you ever heard someone say, "God, listen to me!" in prayer, let alone tell God that he has abandoned them? Yet, David was considered a man after God's own heart because he never let his circumstances come between him and the Lord. Instead he took his circumstances to the Lord. Then he would round out his prayer by declaring who God was, almost as if to say, "These are my circumstances but I remember who you are, Lord."

As I've thought about this kind of processing over the years, I've also wondered why sometimes we feel inhibited expressing ourselves in certain ways that are actually healthy. Why we don't enter the depths of grief we were meant to? Is it because of preconceived ideas of how we should do it? Do we feel it's wrong to express our emotions in certain ways? I think the Bible gives real insight into this if we read Scripture with new eyes.

There will be points in your grief journey that are incredibly difficult as you navigate through your new life. Maybe you don't know what to do with your emotions. Maybe you have questions. Maybe you are angry. Psalm 62:8 says, "Trust in him at all times, you people; pour out your hearts to him; for God is our refuge." Direct it all to him, pour it all out to him.

Even if it feels awkward, refuse to move on until he comes with his presence and you feel something shift in your soul. Let your soul find its refuge in him; refuse to be satisfied with anything else. Then do it day after day. I'm not saying that all your grief will go away, but that's not the point. The point is to connect you more fully to the one who can help you in the middle of your grief. The place of impact in your life will always be the point of connection with him. Seek that connection like you would a treasure.

Going back to the story about Hannah, one of the things that really struck me was just a sidebar in her story. In 1 Samuel 1:4–5 it says, "Whenever the day came for Elkanah to sacrifice, he would give portions of the meat to his wife Peninnah and to all her sons and daughters. But to Hannah he gave a double portion because he loved her." Chances are, if you have experienced loss, there are people around you who, like Elkanah, love you and are kind to you. They hate to see you in turmoil and want to help in any way they can. For Jesse and I it was absolutely like this. We had so many wonderful people who really cared, who cooked for us, gave us gifts, paid for things, and were a huge blessing.

But the thing that stood out to me about Hannah is that she received *some* comfort or favor, but it wasn't *the* comfort. She made it clear that she wasn't going to be satisfied until the Lord himself answered her. That is how it felt for me too. How grateful I was for the love and support from those around us! Honestly it made the load lighter to have others feeling like we did. I often thanked the Lord (and do still today) for kind words and gestures. However, I made it clear to the Lord that I was after something else, something that only came by the Spirit.

As we seek him this way, we will find ourselves becoming a people who carry grief in a different way. I have heard it said that the weight of grief does not become lighter, it's just that you become more equipped and skillful to carry it. That resonates with me and has been my experience as well. However, I would refuse to move on and just glaze over my emotions. Every time I felt the old feeling bubble up again, I would pour it out before the Lord. I would tell him over and over again that I didn't want a spiritual bandage from Him. I needed him to bring deep, real help.

Questions to Ponder:

1. Are there certain expressions of grief you feel uneasy sharing with the Lord? Why?

2. How can you use the examples of Hannah, the Psalmists, and others in the Bible to take the limits off your prayers and make your grief an offering?

3. Read through a few Psalms and find one or two that resonate with you. How can you turn these words into a prayer of your own?

A Prayer in the Processing

Lord, I thank you that your Word says I can come before you boldly and pour out my heart to you. It also says you are close to the brokenhearted. I am counting on that, Lord. I am bringing my turmoil, my hurt and hang-ups to you right now. I recognize you as the Comforter, help me not to hold anything back from you. Fill me as I lift up my prayer to you. You are my help and my salvation, and I look to you.

In Jesus's name, amen.

Chapter 10

Saying Yes to God's Picture

*Be careful that you vigorously maintain God's perspective, and re-
member that it must be done every day, little by little. Don't think
of a finite level. No outside power can touch the proper perspective.*
— Oswald Chambers, *My Utmost for His Highest*

In Scripture, God gives us the recurring symbol of the "picture."

Eden was a picture of heaven when it was created, which is why it was
so devastating when the picture was marred by Adam and Eve's sin. The
earthly tabernacle was a picture of the heavenly tabernacle, which was
why the specifications given to Moses had to be followed to the letter.
Paul speaks about how to conduct oneself in marriage, because marriage
is a picture of Christ and the Church. Taken down to the personal level,
believers are a picture of who God says he is on earth. What happens
when tragedy interrupts our lives and seems to mar that picture and
seemingly contradict every outcome we would expect? As it turns out,
modern day believers were not the only ones who were challenged by
this.

John the Baptist was a New Testament prophet and a cousin to Jesus.
He had been set apart as a Nazarite from birth. He had never cut his hair,

nor had he ever drunk a drop of wine. Basically he had lived the life of an Old Testament prophet, all for the purpose of preparing the way for the "One who was greater" than him. This culminated in John's baptism of Jesus, the starting point of Jesus's ministry!

However, things did not pan out for John as you might think it would. The Bible tells us that after Jesus's baptism, John ended up in prison due to a dispute with a local ruler while Jesus was going throughout towns and villages doing miracles. Matthew 11:2–6 says: "When John, who was in prison, heard about the deeds of the Messiah, he sent his disciples to ask him, "Are you the one who is to come, or should we expect someone else?" Jesus replied, "Go back and report to John what you hear and see: The blind receive sight, the lame walk, those who have leprosy are cleansed, the deaf hear, the dead are raised, and the good news is proclaimed to the poor. Blessed is anyone who does not stumble on account of me."

Wasn't Jesus going to ascend to the throne of David and rule over all? Weren't those closest to him going to be part of that? If so, why was the cousin of Jesus, who had heralded his ministry, rotting in a prison? This was not the picture John had envisioned. The amazing thing to me is that Jesus did not fall all over himself to explain why this was. He basically said, "Here is the evidence that I am who I say I am. Do you still believe it despite your circumstances?"

In another account in Matthew 19:16–22, a man approached Jesus and said:

"Teacher, what good thing must I do to get eternal life?" "Why do you ask me about what is good?" Jesus replied. "There is only One who is good. If you want to enter life, keep the commandments." "Which ones?" he inquired. Jesus replied, "You shall not murder, you shall not commit adultery, you shall not steal, you shall not give false testimony, honor your father and mother,' and 'love your neighbor as yourself.'"

The Rich Young Ruler thought he would receive commendation from Jesus for his good behavior, but he walked away sad because the picture Jesus gave him was not the one he expected. I think most of us would have run after the Rich Young Ruler saying, "You don't understand! What you give up will be nothing in comparison to what you gain! Just try it, you'll see!" But Jesus didn't do any of this. He simply presented himself and said, "Despite this being outside of everything you have known, will you still follow?"

Both of these biblical accounts point to pictures that you could say did not align with the main character's expectation. We could even say that their central view of Jesus was challenged because of it. This is exactly where I found myself post-loss. Prior to losing Graham, our lives seemed like a great picture. God had done amazing things in both Jesse's and my lives, individually and as a couple. We were in a thriving faith community surrounded by friends and family. Then when Graham came along, it was the absolute blessing of our lives. We prayed for and blessed that kid whenever we could. I don't think a child could be more celebrated or loved.

Then suddenly he was gone.

As a bereaved parent, I felt like I could relate a little to my interpretation of John the Baptist sitting in prison.

"Lord if you are who you say you are, then why did it turn out for me like this? This isn't what I expected. It's just not a good picture!"

God has a picture for all of our lives, but sometimes the conclusions we draw when things go wrong are less than accurate. God's picture for us is not painted by perfect circumstances or outcomes that match our expectations. Instead they are painted by who we are in, through—and sometimes despite—our circumstances. If that wasn't the case, then we could consider the martyrs the worst personal failures on the face of the earth. Or Jesus for that matter! Of course, those are the most extreme examples, but imagine if Jesus had judged his life by the persecution he received and the hardship he endured. He would have missed the call of God and never gone to the cross. It's the same for us. If we judge our life's picture by our circumstances and don't realize God's purpose is in who we are in those circumstances, then we are going to be in for a rough ride. God never promised perfection; he promised he would be with us in the imperfection, enabling us to endure and persevere.

I believe the call and challenge for all believers who have experienced trauma or loss is the same: in the midst of tragedy, sorrow, and hardship, will we let God restore us into a picture of his choosing? After losing Graham, Jesse and I had opportunities to speak in front of groups of people and to give our testimony. I had a friend who renewed her relationship with the Lord and began attending church again because of what God did through our story. Many others got to see the Lord shine through us for his glory. And how wonderful that is! But it wasn't about grand gestures, social media posts, or how others perceived us. It wasn't even about doing grief a certain way that was pleasing to others. It was about saying yes to God—to being a picture—when we were alone and not sure what to do next. It was about saying yes when we didn't even know what "yes" looked like.

If you only knew how many times I have personally said to the Lord, "Lord, I am sorry I am not very good at this. I don't know what to do, but I'm saying yes to you. Help me, Lord, even when I don't understand. Please don't leave me alone. Remember me. Remember that I'm dust. Remember I'm putting my hope in you." Even now I'm writing with tears because I still say those words sometimes. That is us saying yes even when we don't understand the why. A faith response says "yes" without dictating the how. It's saying yes to him as we are trying to figure out how to even walk out grief. It's not going to be perfect. Some days you are going to stink at it. Other days you are going to feel like maybe, finally you are breaking through. At the end of the day though, it's those little but personal yeses—the one that starts in your heart, right where you are. Those are the ones that God uses to paint a picture that brings restoration and impacts others. The most amazing thing is that it happens completely outside our control and without our direction.

I can say with honesty that those times of being real before the Lord gave me both the most comforting and most terrifying feelings. I would be at the rock bottom of myself, yet I would feel him surround me and tell me that he hadn't forgotten about me, that he was going to help me. Being a control freak, I would sometimes ask, *"God, but how? How can these broken pieces of my heart be put back together again?"* I knew that my life would forever be changed by loss, so going back to "the way things were" was impossible. But I couldn't even picture what restoration looked like in that context. I would wait, giving him a chance to respond. I never heard him respond to that question, but I could feel his smile. He wasn't a bit concerned that I had no idea how he was going to do that work in me. It taught me how to let go of control as I brought my every emotion, my hurt, my instability, and my insufficiency to him. I never felt as though I couldn't ask him anything, but I also had to be okay with the silence as well.

I'll never forget a story I heard from Havilah Cunnington about something called "provenance." Provenance is the history of a piece of artwork, basically a record of ownership. In her story she told of a valuable painting that had sustained some pretty significant damage in an accident. One would think that after the damage the painting would be worthless, or at least decrease in value. However, in the hands of a master restorer, the painting would actually be repaired and the damage would become part of the artwork's history . . . or provenance. Not only would the painting retain the value, but the restoration would actually add to the story that reinforced its value. So it is with those of us who put ourselves in the hands of the Master Restorer. God will not only repair you; you will find that he enriches the picture of your life in ways that only he can. Yes, the grief will still be there, but so will the picture of restoration. If there is only one thing you can do, say yes!

It took some time, but as I continued to bring my yes to the Lord, I found that he began to do a transforming work in my heart. It honestly went beyond my understanding, much like Ephesians 3:20 says: "Now to him who is able to do immeasurably more than all we ask or imagine, according to his power that is at work within us." I don't know about you, but I can think pretty big! I think this verse is more about being surprised about how God brings things about. When I think about the amazing stories from the Old and New Testament, I realize that he is actually a very creative God! Think about the Israelites being rescued from Egypt after a flurry of miracles. Or about one-hundred-year-old Abraham and ninety-year-old Sarah having a son. Or about Joseph being promoted out of prison into Egyptian leadership. These are very creative outcomes brought about by God, but they required a yes from humans. They had to allow God to work through their circumstances and not give up. Remember, that verse does not say he does immeasurably more "according to God's ability" it says "... according to his power at work in us."

As we submit our lives and grief journeys to the Lord—no matter what they look like, and even if we don't fully know what we're doing all the time—he begins to restore us and paint a picture for his glory. The amazing thing is that even if we are feeling clueless and come to God anyways, he begins to light up the path in front of us. What initially feels like work suddenly becomes intuitive and honestly full of joy! We have to determine to continue to bring our yes to God. As we do, God begins to light up the path for us and clarity comes as we submit our journeys to him. It doesn't require you to emulate someone else you've seen. God wants to take you on your own journey of restoration. Say yes, and you will watch in amazement about how he creatively works in your heart.

Questions to Ponder

1. What part of your picture are you having the most trouble with?

2. How do you see God transforming and restoring your picture for his glory?

A Prayer in the Processing

Lord, I say yes to becoming a picture of your choosing. You are the Master Restorer and I put my life in your hands. I want to be a picture for your glory, even as I am walking through grief. I want to see my life's picture as you do. I need your eyes, not mine!

Just as you creatively walked the patriarchs through trouble and hardship and brought forth a promise, I know you are doing the same for me as I walk through grief with you. Help me to approach you boldly. I look to you and rely on you, Lord. In Jesus's name, amen.

Chapter 11

Grieving in Family

Y ou know, my parents went through this same thing. It's really difficult because you and your spouse will probably process grief in different ways, but you need to be patient with each other. Unfortunately, my parents got divorced because of their loss."

Over the years this phrase, spoken by a colleague, has repeated in my mind. I can confirm that processing grief together with someone else is incredibly challenging. Sometimes you are just trying to survive and the feelings your spouse experiences in their own process can feel like an additional burden. Jesse and I didn't always do it perfectly, but we learned over time how to process grief together, while on very different journeys.

If you can't tell by now, I tended to do more outward processing. Feelings of grief and overwhelming emotion would usually drive me to place where I could pray and express that grief. I would look at pictures and photos on my phone when I was missing Graham and wanted to feel close to him. For Jesse, inadvertently seeing the photos on my phone or hearing me watch a video at a distance was incredibly painful. I would regularly go into Graham's room, while Jesse had a hard time even looking that direction.

Where I processed more outwardly (and probably loudly), Jesse took up a position of quiet and rest. I will be honest, it bothered me because I would compare it to my own processing, and to me it seemed unhealthy.

But the comparison was the problem.

On top of that I started to think thoughts like: *If I let go of every-thing, our marriage would just come crashing down.* Or, *At least I'm letting my emotions out; he's not even processing.* When we finally did talk about it, I had gotten myself to the point of feeling frustrated and alone be-cause of my perception that he wasn't dealing with grief or that he was leaving our marriage to the wayside.

However, what I saw as unhealthy or pain avoidant was actually Jesse processing in his own way, at his own pace, and mostly privately in ways that weren't always visible to me. Not to say that he didn't show emotion, but Jesse was more like a pain camel. Grief would build up for some time and then he would release it all at once. Just because I felt like I had a near-faucet of processing going at all times, that did not mean that he had to process the same way.

After discussing it with Jesse, God revealed to me that the friction was coming from my trust. Did I trust God to walk us both through this together? Did I trust Jesse to know that his grief journey looked different than mine, but different didn't mean that he was letting go of God? I was very honest about my feelings and Jesse was as well. In the end, we understood that we are two different people who process in very different ways, and we need to be patient with each other.

That said, it's important to not invalidate how you feel because of your differences in processing emotions. I could have easily said to my-self, "Natalie, everyone processes differently. You just need to deal with it and move on." Yes, it's important to recognize differences, but it's equally important to talk about your thoughts, questions, and concerns with your spouse constructively. Don't be quick to shove down your own feelings to spare theirs, but also don't use your own grief processing as a template for what is "right." When understanding and supporting each other is your goal, it creates an environment that is helpful and clarifying and that brings healing and greater closeness. It's something Jesse and I had to learn together. It takes patience with each other and a commitment to walking through it together.

Even with this preset as our foundation, we knew our marriage was going to be tested. If you look at statistics on the divorce rate of those who have experienced the loss of a child, it is not pretty. This is something that we talked to each other about often. We agreed that divorce, which was not on the table before we lost Graham, would continue to be off the table. We were going to walk this grief journey together, even if we didn't exactly know what that looked like.

We also agreed to transparency: if we were feeling disconnected we were going to talk about it and, most importantly, pray with each other about it! I truly believe the most important thing about processing with your spouse is agreeing to transparency and facing things together, head on. The one caveat to this is also understanding when we were supposed to go to the Lord, and when we were supposed to go to each other.

Even though Jesse and I processed grief in different ways personally, we found that visiting Graham's plot at the cemetery was a good point of connection as a couple. We would work together to clean and polish his headstone, cut back encroaching grass, and make sure his flower bouquet was fresh. We would also find out that friends and family had been there to visit him, leaving behind little toys, cleaning the headstone themselves, and even planting grass seed on any sparse areas. This was a good time for both of us to let down emotionally and cry.

We would also talk to Graham during those times. It would always start the same: "Hey, buddy." Then we would tell him how much we loved him, how much we missed him, and how much we wished he was here. No matter what though, we always ended it with a kiss on his little picture on his headstone.

I encourage you to find points of connection like these that you and your spouse or family can process together. Everyone processes differently and needs room to do that, but it's equally important to find something to do together. I once saw a video on social media that showed four kids sitting on a couch together, "talking" to their dad who had just passed a few weeks prior.

Maybe it looks like that for you, or maybe it's setting time aside to look through old pictures together. Maybe it's talking about funny things your loved one used to do. Maybe it's independently journaling and talking about it together. Sometimes it's not even about having a set plan but communicating openly with your family and asking them if there is a way they would like to "remember" together.

Even as we were seeking greater connection with each other, Jesse and I were able to connect with another couple who we saw visiting a headstone not far from Graham's spot. Not wanting to encroach on their private time, we waited until they had gone and walked over to the headstone to see who they were visiting. We sighed. They were bereaved parents too. Their precious little girl, named Willow, had only been about three when she passed. Wanting to make a connection with them somehow, I wrote a little card and left it in a plastic bag with a rock on top of the headstone. In it I introduced ourselves and Graham and expressed our condolences for their loss. To our delight they wrote back that next week using the same delivery system we had! We found out that not only were they believers, but the husband had served Jesse at our local Starbucks a few times—and had recognized him at the cemetery. It was a small world! They shared with us that their little girl had passed away from a genetic disorder. As tragic as it was, they said that the doctors had been amazed she had lived that long. She shared that, as parents, they felt blessed by the gift of more time. They also shared that they were currently expecting and they were praying that their new little one would not have the same issue. Beyond leaving a response note, we did not further correspond. However, Jesse and I continued to pray for them and their baby.

I love what Ecclesiastes 4:12 says: "Though one may be overpowered, two can defend themselves." Teamwork in grief is required! As I mentioned in a previous chapter, the enemy would like nothing more than to bring as much isolation and destruction into your life as possible. He will throw every voice possible, trying to put any wedge he can between you and your loved one. Don't take the bait. Be aware that he doesn't attack in obvious ways. In marriage specifically, he probably won't lead in with something way more subversive, like:

"You should get a divorce." He starts with "You know, your spouse just doesn't understand." "They don't feel this like you feel this."

"They're not putting in the work that you are."

"They have become a different person now that_____is gone." "Don't they know that I'm hurting too?"

"It's just easier to disengage."

He wants to start you off on the path of isolation, then create a spiritual stronghold that introduces strife and as much destruction as possible. If he can get you to take the bait with your mind, then speak or act out on his suggestion, you are on the path to being overpowered. This is his tactic 100 percent of the time. Don't fall for it!

Satan will even try to use physical intimacy as a wedge between you and your spouse if he can. I remember the Lord speaking to me specifically about intimacy after we lost Graham. That was not to become a stronghold or an issue in our marriage because of grief.

Unfortunately, I have heard of marriages falling apart after losing a child because this becomes an issue, or old doors to pornography get opened back up again. Talk about this with your spouse. There really should not be any "off the table" topics that you feel like you can't address. Being a couple who walks together through grief takes effort, but if you decide to do it as a team, you will be able to defend yourselves. On top of that, your closeness will grow!

Jesse and I didn't do everything perfectly, but we decided that we were going to submit to the process of walking out grief together. We knew there would be differences in how we processed and perceived things individually. That was okay. What was not okay was resentment building up toward the other person. It was also not okay to play the blame game. We were two hurt people who needed God's help, but we would not be directing that hurt at each other.

If you're reading this and feeling that you are incapable of this— perhaps you don't feel like you have the emotional equity or are overwhelmed—then it's time to talk to someone. First reach out to a spiritual mentor or pastor. These people should be spiritually mature and full of the Holy Spirit. Personally, Jesse and I received so much edification and help from spiritual mentors at church, his parents being the foremost of these. They, too, went through the loss of a son to a car accident and had walked the journey with the Lord and with each other.

Secondly, if you need therapy, get it! Go together if you can. There have been several times in the past few years that Jesse and I have discussed therapy. Did we think we needed it?

Were we feeling any hiccups in our processing that we needed a professional's help to overcome? We both agreed that we could go to therapy at any time either of us felt like we wanted or needed it, and that we would go together. If you feel like you need to go, then let your spouse know how you feel and go. Maybe even if they don't feel the need, it is so healthy to be supportive of the other person and try to help give them whatever it is they need to handle grief in healthy ways. The goal is always to walk away from a therapy session with tools in your tool belt that you can pull out later. That is why having a therapist who not only is a believer but is also filled with the Holy Spirit is so important. The Bible says we don't fight using the same weapons that the world does. Find a therapist who not only wields practical tools but who also understands spiritual weapons.

I also feel compelled to mention prescription medication. Author, speaker, and influencer Carlos Whittaker once summed up his own prior prescription medication usage to help with depression/anxiety perfectly: "It's a help, not my hope." Sometimes we need prescription medication as a help to get us out of a rut, while understanding it is not our ultimate hope of healing. When we walk into it with that mindset, we can leave the door open for God to continue his work in our hearts. Sometimes we need physical help and that's okay! But be cautious if you are just seeking it to numb pain. It's human nature to want a buffer for our uncomfortable emotions, but processing pain will happen one way or another. Be wary of the things that present themselves as a way to get around this, including alcohol and other substances. We know our own hearts; be transparent about it with your spouse, mentors, and therapist.

Ultimately each person's grief journey is between them and the Lord, but we walk the road with those closest to us. How we cooperate with each other is an important part of processing. There is nothing that has a greater potential to frustrate us. Conversely there is nothing that has a greater capacity to provide comfort to us. May we determine in our hearts that we are going to be "a strand of two cords" so that we are not overwhelmed by the enemy's schemes. Let's place our hope and our expectation on the Lord, not on how we perceive someone else's grief journey. When we do this, each finds freedom to grieve and process how the Lord has called us to—creating a strength that cannot be overcome!

Questions to Ponder

1. How do you and your closest loved ones process grief differently?

2. What opportunities are there to process together?

A Prayer in the Processing

Father, I bring my and my family's lives before you. Help us to process grief individually and together in healthy ways. Lead me by your Spirit and help me to know when to speak and when to stay silent. Help us talk about our differences in constructive ways that bring understanding and grace. Lord, I know it's you who holds us together. Hold us in your hand and draw us close to you as we walk this out. In Jesus's name, amen.

Chapter 12

Grieving in a Community

And let us consider how we may spur one another on toward love and good deeds, not giving up meeting together, as some are in the habit of doing, but encouraging one another—and all the more as you see the Day approaching.

—Hebrews 10:24–25

Gathering in community is important. So important, in fact, that the writer of Hebrews mentions it specifically—don't forsake it! This is just as important after loss as it is before. Even if up to this point you haven't been a regular church attender or have been more of an online person, I encourage you to find a body that you can connect with in person. So many amazing and life-changing things can happen in the real-time interactions of God's saints gathered together. If you've walked away dissatisfied with your church experience so far, then let me encourage you that it's because you haven't found the right place. Let me assure you: it exists! When you find it, it's worth the inconvenience of driving long distances, or even moving across the country to be in community there.

The point is: find a place where you can be spiritually fed. You need a place where you are challenged to grow and receive good spiritual training. A place where the power and the fruit of the Holy Spirit is seen. I have often heard that the three-stranded cord was about two people and God, and I think that is a great picture. However, I believe there is a personal and communal element to that third strand. We need a personal relationship with him, but we also need the strength that comes from being part of a body of believers.

When Graham passed away, Jesse and I were surrounded by friends, family, and church family who knew the Scripture "rejoice with those who rejoice; mourn with those who mourn." We found ourselves surrounded by a community who truly grieved with us, cared for us, and prayed for us. It really ministered to us. There were people who said, "I am so sorry. I don't even know what to say; it just hurts." It's okay to not have all the words. Many of them were also reeling from the suddenness of our loss. We had brought Graham to church the whole fourteen months he was with us, so many had made a connection with him. I remember someone saying that it made them sad that they never got a chance to fight for Graham in prayer because of the suddenness of his passing. People brought us meals and gifts and were so kind and supportive. Our amazing work community even set up a Go Fund Me to offset funeral expenses, something that blessed us tremendously and allowed us to spare no expense when it came to Graham's funeral arrangements.

More than just kind words though, it really was something of beauty to watch the Lord minister to us through and in the midst of the people we knew in meaningful and personal ways. There have been more instances than I can count of people who have had an encouraging, comforting, or prophetic word at the right moment. I'm not talking about generic platitudes.

Oftentimes they spoke right to where we were, and it was the word we needed. I think the biggest impact though, and one that I can't emphasize enough, was the fact we could walk into a church where we could receive solid teaching in the Word combined with the ministry of the Holy Spirit. It was absolutely the context we needed for healthy grief processing.

For those who have walked through grief, you know that even after having experienced it, not everything is about grief. In the process of grief, though, a lot of things come up and stem from it. Past hurts, traumas, character flaws, your own humanity, and feeling overwhelmed. So much of this is just life stuff that is magnified by grief. Being in a place where we could experience the presence of God with a group of people seeking him with all their hearts was a crucial environment we needed and a pivotal part of our journey.

Maybe, like us, you were in a body of believers and an environment of transformation and healing. But maybe you weren't or aren't. If you are currently in a church where you are not experiencing the overwhelming and life-changing presence of God, then find one where you can. Your church may be a good church that preaches the Word of God, but if the connection with the Holy Spirit is missing then so will be an avenue of God's comfort for you personally. I can't tell you how many times we walked into a church service raw and hurting, and God ministered to us in very personal ways, all while a normal service was going on, oftentimes without anyone mentioning one word about grief.

Jesse and I have always made it our goal to be part of a local church that teaches solid theology and operates in the five-fold ministry where the Holy Spirit is not just acknowledged but embraced in all his biblical expressions. Paul sums it up perfectly when he said that "my message and my preaching were not with wise and persuasive words, but with a demonstration of the Spirit's power" (1 Cor. 2:4). These are places where people's lives are transformed from glory to glory and where growth doesn't stop at prayer of salvation. What we experienced in the body of believers went so far beyond just grief care. Our whole lives were constantly being ministered to, and we had a completely safe environment to worship, to receive, and to fall apart if we needed to.

One of the wonderful things about grieving in a healthy (that doesn't mean perfect!) community is how it opened avenues for God to creatively minister to us. God frequently reached out and brought his comfort in unique ways. Generally our church services consisted of worship, a sermon, and a time to receive prayer after the message. Even before Graham passed it was not uncommon for Jesse and me to go forward to receive prayer as a way to respond to what had been preached and invite the Lord to do more work in our hearts. After Graham, though, we felt even more of a need to have that extra ministry from the Lord. I will never forget one particular Sunday, a few months after Graham passed, when I went forward to receive prayer in response to the message. As the prayer person was praying for me, I could feel the ministry of the Holy Spirit. Suddenly the prayer changed course and she said, "I command the knots in your stomach to be released in Jesus's name." What she didn't know is that ever since Graham passed, it had been very difficult for me to eat. I had almost a constant sense of nausea and "knots" in my stomach that were causing me to lose weight. In that moment, I felt a physical, tangible release in my body. I was amazed because I had not mentioned this to anyone outside of my family! From that point on I had no more issues with nausea and could eat normally.

I mentioned it before, but in the immediate aftermath of Graham's passing we felt a new sensitivity to the Lord and an awareness of him like we had never felt before. There were many times that we sensed the presence of God very closely, or the presence of angelic beings, or even the feeling that Graham could see or hear us. One of the ways that God creatively ministered to Jesse in community was by giving him glimpses of Graham in heaven, often during times of worship. This wasn't something Jesse would seek to contrive, but the Lord in his mercy and kindness would unexpectedly show him these images. When I asked Jesse what Graham looked like, he said that sometimes Graham looked young but other times he looked like a teenager. That didn't make sense in our brains, for obvious reasons. Graham was only fourteen months old when he passed away! However in the book *Imagine Heaven*, John Burke describes stories like these in which people take on different ages at different times, in ways that were impactful for the person seeing into heaven. At the end of the day, we decided not to overanalyze it nor make a theology out of it. We instead decided to receive the creative ministry of the Holy Spirit as he saw fit. Each time God would open up Jesse's eyes, it was at pivotal moments and would bring comfort and a release of sorrow.

Although I did not often see visions of Graham, there were special times during worship especially that I would feel Graham with us, worshipping the Lord—sometimes even coming between us and taking our hands! That may sound crazy to you, but Jesse and I would each, independently feel it! One night about six months after Graham passed, I "saw" him for the first time. We were participating in a worship night at our church. We were in a smaller building, so there were probably about one hundred fifty people there total, all shoved into every nook and cranny of that place. We sang a few different songs, but a particular song was lifting up the name of the Lord and talked about who he is. All of a sudden, in my spirit I saw Graham not far above our heads. He looked to be about four or five years old. He was looking at me and started jumping up and down excitedly and full of joy. "It's all true, Mom! It's all true! Everything you are saying is all true!" he said. I could feel his overwhelming and unrestrained joy. Immediately I felt that same overwhelming joy and wonder. Not just because I saw Graham, but because I knew we were experiencing in part what Graham knew in full. He was seeing the fullness of what we were experiencing in the room. I felt that in that moment we were truly worshipping the Lord together. It is a gift I will always treasure.

Comparing my experiences to Jesse's was interesting at times. I felt as though Jesse was constantly seeing Graham in visions, usually during our worship time at church, whereas a lot of my experiences came in senses and feelings, like a feeling of special closeness to the Lord at certain times. I never relied on the feelings, but this was the way God ministered to me most.

One night I had a dream about Graham that was very vivid. The season leading up to that night had been particularly difficult and emotional for me. In the dream Graham looked to be about two. We were in a large open kitchen together. He was running around like crazy, as toddlers do, and as I watched him, I felt a tangible wave of relief sweep over me. I thought to myself: *Everyone else was so worried and thought he was gone, but here he is safe and sound!* I was sitting on a stool in the middle of the room watching him as he ran energetically in circles around me. During one of his laps, he swung a little closer to me, so I grabbed him and squeezed him so tight. He laughed and laughed, trying to struggle free and get away from my smothering "mommy kisses." In spite of the commotion, I could even feel his chubby cheek pressed up close to mine. When I let go of him, he ran over to the fridge, tapped on it, and looked up and said, "Choc milk."

I repeated back to him, "You want some chocolate milk?"

I got up and opened the door, and then I woke up. It was the first time I dreamed about him, which was comforting. However, the dream had actually imparted something else to me—relief. I feel like God imparted a relief to me that was not of this world but completely supernatural. It wasn't just a mental knowing; it was something I experienced. He gave me eyes to see from heaven's perspective.

Grief hits everyone differently at different times. God was so good to Jesse and me through the people in our lives. Many reached out to encourage us, and they often would tear up while pouring out their hearts. Sometimes I would feel guilty if I also didn't have this uprising of emotion and tears on days when I felt like my emotions had already been "spent." But I learned that everyone has different emotional points; you just have to process them as they come. Don't feel guilty if you don't feel them in every situation. It's not our job to drum up emotions. We can still be thankful and appreciate a kind gesture from someone who cares, even if we're not in the same emotional place at the moment.

Every person is different, so your moments with God will be different as well. I only share these experiences Jesse and I have had to increase your expectation in your own life. We don't rely only on experiences—we rely on and connect with the Lord—but the outworking of that can be receiving God's comfort in unique ways that are especially meaningful for you.

Questions to Ponder

1. Do you feel you are properly connected to a healthy faith community?

2. If yes, what are some ways you have noticed God ministering to you through others?

3. If not, what do you need to do in order to connect to a healthy place of worship?

A Prayer in the Processing

Father, I am so thankful that you created the Body of Christ to function as a unit, so that if one part hurts, the whole body cares for it. Thank you for ministering to me, and showing how you want to minister through others as well. Thank you for comfort in all its forms! Connect me with the right people as I seek not only to be edified myself, but to edify others as well. May you be glorified in every interaction. I love you. In Jesus's name, amen.

Chapter 13

Surrendering to the Comforter

At the time of the writing of this book, it has been a little over six years since our son passed. As I've reflected on the past six years, in some ways it seems like yesterday and in other ways I feel like I have lived a hundred lifetimes. With each passing year we have added a new stone of remembrance to the pile of our lives. Graham has not been forgotten by us.

Grief has changed in those years too. To give you an idea of a timeline, in the beginning Graham was the first thing I thought about in the morning and the last thing I thought about before going to bed at night. Every hour between felt like I was constantly "remembering" my son was no longer here. My grief cup always felt on the verge of spilling over.

Around year three to four, I found there was a little less emotion constantly simmering under the surface. A normalization of sorts happened. What felt like heavy emotional labor in the first years became a little easier to navigate and more intuitive.

Years five and six have been a redefining period for my life as a bereaved parent. I have learned what it looks like, not only to receive God's creative comfort, but also to be part of his giving it to others. I go back to the saying that grief doesn't get any lighter, you just get more skilled in carrying it—because it's true. In my experience, grief has been like a heavy rock held in a cloth bag. At first, the fabric resists the pressure, resenting the bulky weight it has to bear. But over time the fabric begins to relax—to expand

and stretch with the rock's weight to the point that it creates more space inside. By the grace of God, I have found my heart stretching in ways I never thought it could, making room for God to minister.

Even as grief has changed over the years, there are still times when I feel that old familiar feeling welling up inside again. Sometimes it's random. Most times it's around Graham's birthday or his heaven day. Other times I've noticed that when I'm feeling particularly stressed or life gets hectic, those emotions are closer to the surface. I will say that my "grieve, wash, repeat" pattern for processing has never changed. I will sit in the emotion and really feel it. I will cry the tears and tell Graham how much I miss him. Often I will tell him I am so glad he is in heaven and safe, but that I can't wait until I can throw my arms around him and hug and kiss him. Then I will take up my position once again to pour out my heart to the Lord as an offering. Sometimes it's raw and loud. Sometimes it looks more like me telling God that I trust him and I'm standing on his promises. Regardless of how it looks or how I feel, I always receive something from the Lord that washes over me and fills me up. I never leave empty, and I never leave the same. That is the power of God's creative comfort.

If you're going through a particularly tough season, please know that it does get easier. If you feel like you are finding your way with the Lord in your grief journey, I encourage you to lean into Him all the more. Naturally, some of our seasons are linked to time. There will always be hills and valleys in life and it's the same in our grief journeys.

Matthew 5:4 says, "Blessed are those who mourn, for they will be comforted."

What strikes me about this verse is that you can't really receive comfort unless you have felt the lack of it. Those of us who have experienced grief or trauma have certainly felt lack of comfort, haven't we? When

Jesus says you will be comforted, what exactly does he mean? Comforted by whom? Your family? Your neighbor? Sister Betty on the third row? No, we are comforted by God himself.

God's comfort makes even mourning a blessed state. I'm telling you from experience that the blessedness of mourning is like none other. Yes, there is great pain. However, even in the most painful of moments, the comfort of God absolutely overwhelms it. Grief is still there, but it is swallowed up by the Comforter. 1 Corinthians 15:55 says, "Where, O death, is your victory? Where, O death, is your sting?" I used to think of that verse as an excuse not to feel pain. Like, "Death, you ain't got nothing on me!" But that would only be true if death didn't happen; unfortunately, death did and does happen. But as you allow the Lord to work, you will find that it doesn't get to have the final word. It doesn't get to dress you in grave clothes for the rest of your life.

I truly believe that for some of you, what you have read in these pages is confirmation of what God has been impressing upon your heart already. Hope is springing up because you realize that you have been walking the walk without knowing it. For others, this may be a redirection: a revelation that your grief journey is supposed to be more than just getting through. I hope that these pages have filled your mind with possibilities and expanded your God imagination—or at the very least, I hope that it has given you a starting point. God is working and he wants to walk with you and speak to you and encourage you in your grief journey. It goes beyond generic platitudes. God wants to comfort you in creative, unique, and personal ways. He wants to remove the stumbling blocks and hang-ups that stand between you and Himself. He wants you to know him more fully in your grief. He wants to transform you in the wrestle. He wants to restore your life's picture for his glory.

I love this quote by A. W. Tozer from *The Pursuit of God:*

> In our desire after God let us keep always in mind that God also
> has desire, and His desire is toward the sons of men, and more
> particularly toward those sons of men who will make the once-
> for-all decision to exalt Him over all. Such as these are precious
> to God above all treasures of earth or sea. In them God finds a
> theater where He can display his exceeding kindness toward us
> in Christ Jesus. With them God can walk unhindered: toward
> them He can act like the God He is.

What may sound like a grit-your-teeth effort to "exalt him above all"
is actually just surrender. It's placing your grief in the hands of a loving
God and asking him to lead you through it and being determined to
walk it out with him day by day. We must take our hands off the steering wheel of control and realize that we aren't always going to feel like
we know what we're doing. The last part of that quote is probably my
favorite: "with them God can walk unhindered: toward them He can
act like the God He is." When we make the choice to exalt him above
all, to surrender everything, we get to experience God acting toward us
without limitation. It is here we find that his comfort flows to our lives
in creative, unexpected, and transformative ways.

God makes it clear in his Word that he wants to carry our burdens.
He wants to help us in our distress. He wants to bring healing and restoration to our lives. But we can limit his work in our lives if we don't
understand that this process is more than just mental agreement with
God's intention with a "wait and see" approach. There must be revelation knowledge that awakens our hearts, engages our faith in new ways,

and causes us to shake off personal limitations that hold us back from full communion with him. Let's talk about what this surrender looks like in different areas of our lives.

Personal Devotion Time

Personal devotion time is where we feed ourselves spiritually with Bible reading, study, and prayer. It goes beyond just grief processing and into relationship with the Lord. I compare this to a meal. If we find ourselves skipping meals more often than not (or filling ourselves with the wrong things) we can expect physical and psychological symptoms of malnourishment. However when we prioritize communing with the Lord, we find ourselves operating from a place of fullness, which is the ideal context for grief processing. I can tell you from experience, it's better to be full!

This may be the place where most personal uncertainty lies for you. You may be navigating awkwardness, uncertainty, or frustration with your ability to connect with the Lord in meaningful ways. If this is you, there's good news! You have a basis for approaching the Lord—and the words are already provided. Even if you're feeling frustration, uncertainty, awkwardness, whatever emotion—I encourage you to use those words and direct them to God. When we approach the Lord from a place of truth and honesty, you will find him taking those feelings and turning them into something that produces connection with the Lord.

If you're looking for a place to start, first make the decision that you are going to surrender everything to him. Tell the Lord, no matter how it feels, that your intention is to seek him, to exalt him above everything in your life. Be honest about how you feel but reaffirm that you want to know him more and grow your relationship with him. Find verses in the

Bible that talk about the character and nature of God and pray them out loud. Seek out teachings and podcasts that stir up your spiritual hunger. Read books that increase your spiritual vocabulary and inspire prayer. Sometimes our feelings won't feel settled immediately, but you must continue to state your intentions to the Lord and your desire to connect with him more fully. If you feel a lack of desire, tell him you want to desire that connection more! As you do this, you will be amazed at how quickly you will feel his presence flooding your life. The number one thing that has helped me through disconnection in my personal walk is something my pastor in Kansas City would often say: "God loves to be pursued." Hebrews 11:6 says that God "rewards those who earnestly seek him." Make that your aim, and you'll find him rewarding you with greater revelation of and closeness with himself—the greatest treasure of all.

In general I have found myself drawn to two biblical patterns for prayer in my personal devotional time. One of these is the David prayer model, established in Psalms:

- Tell God the problem and how you feel about it.

- Remember and tell the Lord how he's helped you or his people in the past.

- Declare God's nature, ways, character, and promise.

- Declare you are trusting in him and end with thanksgiving.

The other is the model established by Jesus in Luke 11:2–4 when his disciples asked him how to pray:

He said to them, "When you pray, say: 'Father, hallowed be your name, your kingdom come. Give us each day our daily bread. Forgive us our sins, for we also forgive everyone who sins against us. And lead us not into temptation.'"

The prayer itself is pretty straightforward and is wonderful to say as is. As you get more comfortable praying this, you can begin to expound on each part of that prayer. Often I would start by lifting up and exalting the name of the Lord and read from Psalms, declaring his goodness and his character. Then I would ask for him or his kingdom reality to be realized in the circumstance or for the person I was praying for. This is also a good place to declare specific promises from the Word.

Then I would ask him for what I needed. I would then ask him to forgive me of my sins, I would release everyone who had sinned against me, and I would specifically name things or people if needed. Finally, I asked him to lead me in his ways and to light the path in front of me as I sought to lean, not on my own understanding, but to acknowledge him in all I did.

I hope that as you're reading this you are getting ideas of how you can move forward in your personal devotion time. As mentioned, there is a resource guide where I have listed my personal favorite devotionals and books that have built my faith. Maybe there are others that you have found that really encourage you. Dive in! Realize that as you deepen your prayer life, this won't always feel like second nature. That's okay! Be patient with yourself and determined to wait on the Lord. Like most things in life, we get more comfortable the more we practice.

Church

It is so very important to gather regularly in community—to know others and be known in a communal setting. Like the passage in Ephesians,

I liken it to a physical body. A body part that is not attached to the body is cut off from life-giving nourishment that the body provides. Does that mean the body is perfect and has no issues? Not at all. No matter what particular body of believers you find yourself in, there will always be imperfections because it's made up of humans. I once heard someone say, "The body of Christ ceased to be perfect the moment I joined it." It's so true! Despite those imperfections though, God does amazing and wonderful things in a group of imperfect people who are "seeking first the kingdom of God and his righteousness." Hebrews 6:1 charges us to "move beyond the elementary teachings about Christ and be taken forward to maturity." Finding a place that can nourish you with spiritual milk then graduate you into spiritual meat should be your goal—whether it be a small church, big church, or home church. When you find it, I would challenge you not only to be an attender but someone who invests your time, energy, and finances as outlined in Scripture. As we seek connection in community, we not only become edified, but also bring edification to others in turn.

One of the most memorable examples of this happened about a year ago. I was having a really rough week personally. I was simultaneously missing Graham, dealing with some health issues, and struggling after finding out that I was not pregnant. I was in my closet crying to the Lord out of pure hurt and frustration. I still missed Graham. How long would it be? Is there something more we should be doing? Remember us, Lord! Lots of questions, lots of petitions and tears, lots of pouring out my heart to the Lord. In true Psalmist form though, I ended my time with thanksgiving. I thanked the Lord that he heard and saw us, that he was not slow to fulfill his promises, that he was a God of his Word, that I was trusting him. As I was cleaning up my face in the bathroom afterward, I thought to myself, *If someone says something to me about this, about our future, or gives me a word . . . then I will know God sees me.* Then I kind of laughed at myself because our lives looked pretty good from the outside. No one would know the kind of anguish I had been going through lately.

The next week, our church hosted a Zoom prayer meeting in which several couples, including Jesse and I, were called upon to pray. I had forgotten about that moment in the bathroom and was trying my best to shake off the funk of the past week. It was another couple's turn to pray before us, and we expected them to get right into it. Instead the woman stopped and said she had a word for someone on the call—for me! She then proceeded to say the following, which she wrote down for me later:

> The pain of your journey is known and seen by your God. It's not wasted and it's not for nothing. Hold on. He has more for you; he is preparing you. He sees all that you have yielded to him already, but he wants it all—all of you. I believe he wants it all so he can fully prepare you, not a burden for you to carry but as a release. Get ready, be prepared, he's about to pour out.

The rest of the word was about the future, which I don't need to detail here but which addressed everything I had poured out to the Lord that day in my closet. He was saying, "Stay the course. I'm working. I haven't forgotten you." In that moment I felt the words of Hagar in Genesis resonate in my spirit. After the angel of the Lord spoke comforting words to her, Genesis 16:13 says, "She gave this name to the LORD who spoke to her, You are the God who sees me." Like that night in Zurich, I knew the Lord had seen me, and in that moment it was all I needed.

There are more moments like this than I can possibly capture in one book, but the point is that God wants to minister to you in and through community. Proverbs 18:1 says, "A man who isolates himself . . . rages against all wise judgment" (NKJV). In short, those who isolate themselves fail. In my years in community I have seen this truth play out time and again. I don't want that to be you! Make every effort to get plugged in somewhere, even if it challenges you. Ask the Holy Spirit to guide you to the right place, and he will!

Be aware of the traps of the enemy as you are doing this, especially if you are dealing with past church hurt. You could say Jesus was hurt most by his own people, yet he chose to die for them. This was not a place of victimhood but of victory for him. If you find yourself constantly feeling victimized in community, then it's time to have an honest conversation with a trusted mature believer who is committed to a local body of believers. If you don't know anyone like this, ask someone for a connection or find a counselor like this. Whatever you do, don't allow any lie of the enemy or any stronghold of hurt to stand between you and edification from the body of Christ. More than you individually, the enemy hates the body of Christ and does everything in his power to keep us from each other.

Personal Relationships

Finally, it's time to do a relationship check. In addition to personal and communal edification, it is also important to have people around you with whom you can be completely honest about how you're doing. Thankfully Jesse and I had several in our immediate family, as well as close friends and pastors, with whom we could be completely transparent and felt the freedom to fall apart if we needed to. They played a key role in encouraging us and praying with us during particularly challenging times. My parents-in-law, who had tragically gone through the loss of an adult son themselves about fifteen years prior, were a wonderful sounding board for Jesse and I as we navigated grief. One piece of advice my father-in-law gave us was about sharing with others, and he told us we needed to realize that some people aren't in the place to go there with you. This may be due a lack of relational capital, or perhaps they are going through a battle themselves. Telling them about something so precious as loss will leave you feeling emptier than you did before. Even with this advice, I have unfortunately experienced this a time or two in my grief journey, and I have left conversations kicking myself for having opened my mouth. There is nothing worse than spilling your guts to someone who just can't "go there" with you. That is why it is so important to find trusted people in whom you can confide and from whom you can receive encouragement.

Depending on how healthy your family environment is, these people may or may not be directly related to you. The point is not to feel bad or make anyone else feel bad, but rather to honestly assess your relationships and realize that not everyone can be a confidante. God can use even those who have not gone through loss themselves to minister to you. God used people who did and did not go through loss to minister to Jesse and me in powerful ways. If you are looking around at those closest to you and feel like you lack this kind of outlet, seek a good connection at church (a mentor/pastor) or a Spirit-filled counselor. The point is to get connected with someone who is a stable believer, full of the Holy Spirit, with good fruit in their lives.

Conclusion

Therefore, since we are surrounded by such a great cloud of witnesses, let us throw off everything that hinders and the sin that so easily entangles. And let us run with perseverance the race marked out for us, fixing our eyes on Jesus, the pioneer and perfecter of faith.

Hebrews 12:1–2

After Graham passed, this verse took on new meaning. I have often heard it said that those who have passed on in the Lord get to join the great cloud of heavenly witnesses who are watching us on earth below. I think the writer of Hebrews meant it to be a motivational: "Remember who has gone before you, let it keep you sober-minded and focused." However, one day I got a spiritual picture of what it could actually look like up there. I saw runner after runner crossing a finish line, their arms and heads lifted in overwhelming joy that they had completed what they set out to do. They had finished! I fully expected them to leave the course to enjoy their rest, but instead each one turned back to join those on the sidelines, cheering on their friends and family who were still running. They were saying things like: "You got this! Don't stop, keep going. Almost there! Don't give up!"

Then it hit me. That is the great cloud of witnesses cheering us on. Those we know and love who have crossed the finish line and have a complete heavenly perspective are telling us it's worth it, to not give up, to finish strong. They are now seeing in real time that which we are participating in faith. If we only realized how many eyes are on us, voices cheering us on, telling us it's worth it. That he is worth it. These are people who have left earthly cares behind and have communion with the One we are living for. We can only see through our earthly eyes, but they have gained a new viewpoint.

Let that motivate you. Picture your loved one cheering you on. They have no more sorrow, no more tears. Only fullness of joy and a keen interest in watching those they love finish strong. My friends, we have our whole lives ahead of us to run. Let me echo what those in the great crowd of witnesses are saying "Don't give up, keep pressing into Him!"

I love what L. B. Cowman wrote in *Streams in the Desert*, which we received as a gift after Graham passed away:

> A distinguished general related this pathetic incident of his own experience in time of war. The general's son was a lieutenant of battery. An assault was in progress. The father was leading his division in a charge; as he pressed on in the field, suddenly his eye was caught by the sight of a dead battery-officer lying just before him. One glance showed him it was his own son. His fatherly impulse was to stop beside the loved form and give vent to his grief, but the duty of the moment demanded that he should press on in the charge; so quickly snatching one hot kiss from the dead lips, he hastened away leading his command in the assault. You are in the line of battle, and the crisis is at hand. To falter a moment would be to imperil some Holy interest. Other lives would be harmed by your pausing; Holy interests would suffer, should your hands be folded. Sorrow makes deep scars; it

writes its record ineffaceably on the heart, which suffers. There is a humanizing and fertilizing influence in sorrow, which has been rightly accepted and cheerfully borne. Indeed, they are poor who have never suffered, and have none of sorrow's marks upon them. The joy set before us will shine upon our grief as the sun shines through the clouds, glorifying them. God has so ordered, that in pressing on in duty we shall find the truest, richest comfort for ourselves. Light will come again, and we shall grow stronger.[4]

In the past several years I have probably read that excerpt a few hundred times. It has influenced and inspired the way I have walked through grief. I can attest to the part that says: "God has so ordered that in pressing on in duty we shall find the truest, richest comfort for ourselves. Light will come again, and we shall grow stronger." Yes, we have pressed on in duty in the midst of sorrow, but it has been our continual pressing into the Lord, keeping our eyes fixed on him, that has made all the difference for us. We made that our duty. It's not about overcoming grief (as if that were possible), it has—and always will be—about seeking the only One who can help us through it. I can say in truth that we have experienced rich comfort from the Lord, and we have grown stronger. Even in the midst of sorrow, there is a joy set before us, if only we will seek the Lord.

CONCLUSION

Questions to Ponder

1. How do you feel God calling you to surrender more in personal devotion time, community, and personal relationships?

2. How have you noticed God ministering to you in personal or creative ways in the midst of grief?

3. What are some of your top takeaways or "aha moments" from this book?

A Prayer in the Processing:

Father, thank you for speaking to me. Thank you for showing me how you want to pour out your creative comfort in my life. I give up control and open up my heart for you to surprise me in my grief journey! I surrender every hang-up that has kept me from communing with you, the body of Christ, and being in edifying relationships. May you be exalted above all in my life as I seek you. May I not only receive your comfort, but be someone who pours it out to others.

In Jesus's name, amen!

Recommended Resources

My Favorite Daily Reading Devotionals:

Chambers, Oswald. *My Utmost for His Highest.* Our Daily Bread Publishing, 2023.

Cahn, Jonathan. *The Book of Mysteries.* Frontline Books, 2016.

Great Resources to Study and Build Foundational Theology:

Breen, Mike. *Covenant and Kingdom: The DNA of the Bible.* Pawleys Island, SC: 3DMPublishing, 2010.

McKnight, Scot, *The King Jesus Gospel: The Original Good News.* Grand Rapids, MI: Zondervan, 2016.

Morphew, Derek, *Breakthrough: Discovering the Kingdom.* Cape Town, South Africa: Vineyard International Publishing, 2019.

Wright, N. T., *The Kingdom New Testament.* Grand Rapids, MI: Zondervan, 2012.

—*Interpreting Scripture: Essays on the Bible and Hermeneutics.* Grand Rapids, MI: Zondervan, 2020.

RECOMMENDED RESOURCES

Books to Inspire Faith and Fuel Prayer:

Bolz, Shawn, *Breakthrough: Prophecies, Prayers and Declarations.* Studio City, CA: ICreate Productions, 2019.

—*Translating God: Hearing God's Voice for Yourself and the World Around You.* Studio City, CA: ICreate Productions, 2015.

Capps, Charles, *The Tongue: A Creative Force.* Tulsa, OK: Harrison House, 1995.

Tozer, A. W. *The Pursuit of God.* Harrisburg, PA: Christian Publications, Inc, 1948, 2015.

—*The Knowledge of the Holy.* New York: HarperCollins, 1961, 2009.

—*God's Pursuit of Man.* Chicago: Moody Publishers, 1950, 1978.

Notes

1. John Burke, *Imagine Heaven: Near-Death Experiences, God's Promises, and the Exhilarating Future That Awaits You* (Grand Rapids, MI: Baker, 2015), 29.
2. Oswald Chambers, *My Utmost for His Highest.* Our Daily Bread Publishing, 2023.
3. N. T. Wright, *Simply Good News: Why the Gospel Is News and What Makes It Good* (New York: HarperOne, 2017), 137.

IF YOU ENJOYED THIS BOOK,
PLEASE CONSIDER SHARING IT WITH OTHERS.

Recommend this book personally to friends and family, as well as to those in your small group, book club, workplace, and classes.

Mention the book in a blog post or on Twitter, or upload a photo of the cover with your positive review to Instagram, Facebook, and Pinterest.

Connect with the author on Facebook to express your appreciation for the book's message and, perhaps, how it had a positive effect on your life.

Order a copy of the book for someone you know who would be challenged and encouraged by its message.

Look for the book on Amazon.com and leave a positive review.

And visit us to see the many other books, products, and publishing services we offer.

CreativeEnterprisesStudio.com

1507 SHIRLEY WAY, SUITE A
BEDFORD, TX 76022-6737
ACREATIVESHOP@AOL.COM

131

Made in the USA
Columbia, SC
11 December 2024

48935117R00083